Uncover the Extraordinary Opportunities That Lead to Business Breakthroughs

 **res • o • na • tor** [rez-*uh*-ney-ter]
—*noun*

1. the perfect solution to a specific problem.
2. a product or service so powerful it sells itself.
3. an offering that connects to what your market values most.
4. an idea that people immediately understand has value to them.

Tuned In shows you six simple, yet powerful steps to creating products, services, or ideas that resonate. Getting tuned in is a process anyone can master and no business can afford to ignore.

Praise for *Tuned In*

"When was the last time you bought a product and said, 'I've got to tell my friends!'? This book will change the way you look at success and failure in the marketplace. When companies think they know what their customers need, it invariably ends badly. But for those who spend the time to really understand the problems potential customers have, success often awaits. I recommend *Tuned In* to anyone who is looking for a guidebook on how to uncover the obvious opportunities that others do not see."

—*Rob McGovern, Founder of CareerBuilder.com,*
Chairman and CEO, Jobfox.com

"Wow. I learned something on every page. I'm convinced the *Tuned In* strategy will work for anyone who has a breakthrough product, service, company, or cause. The authors make the compelling argument that most marketers focus on traditional and ineffective steps to reach the customer. But success in the marketplace demands that common myths be exposed and replaced with new thinking on how to create and pitch products and services. As a communications coach, I will use these concepts with my clients to help them become 'resonators' who stand out from their competitors."

—*Carmine Gallo, Communications Coach,*
author of Fire Them Up!

"*Tuned In* is the perfect playbook for aspiring corporate and life champions. It presents an unshakeable foundation from which to build greatness. The principles of this great work serve as a compass for keeping our ministry focused as we move from season to season on this great journey.

—*David L. Cook, Founder Links of Utopia Ministries*
and author of Golf's Sacred Journey

"You can keep guessing what will lead to your big business break-throughs, or . . . you can read this book, tune in, and turn on extraordinary results. Highly recommended."

—Michael Port, Author of Book Yourself Solid
and Beyond Booked Solid

"The most important thing a CEO has to do is make sure his or her company is and stays tuned in. There are ongoing challenges with people, culture, strategy, and execution, but the real difference maker is consistently producing products and services the market loves. This book provides a simple process all CEO's should adopt to help make sure their teams are focused on the most important things that drive success."

—Steve Bennett, Retired CEO of Intuit

"This is a unique and fresh approach to how fortunes are made today."

—Rick Page, Author of the #1 sales bestseller,
Hope Is Not a Strategy

"Far too many product and marketing managers go about their daily work without understanding the fundamentals of creating a market-driven business. *Tuned In* offers a proven methodology in an easy-to-understand format filled with real-world examples we all can relate to. It's like a marketing cookbook, but one that instantly makes us experts."

—Nilofer Merchant, CEO, Rubicon Consulting

"The music industry has been completely 'tuned out,' not only to their customers, but even more so to the artists whom they claim to represent. For the artists that we represent, and the fans (customers) that we want to reach, *Tuned In* is a great reminder of what so many established stars, and those on their way, already know; 'Find out what your fans want, and then find a way to give it to them.'"

—Jody Nachtigal, Personal Manager at Arcadia Group Management and
Co-President of record label, Kissing Booth Music

Tuned In

Tuned In

Uncover the Extraordinary
Opportunities That Lead to
Business Breakthroughs

Craig Stull, Phil Myers, and David Meerman Scott

WILEY

John Wiley & Sons, Inc.

Published by John Wiley & Sons, Inc., Hoboken, New Jersey
Published simultaneously in Canada

For general information on our other products and services or for technical support, please contact our Customer Care Department within the United States at (800) 762-2974, outside the United States at (317) 572-3993 or fax (317) 572-4002.

Wiley also publishes its books in a variety of electronic formats. Some content that appears in print may not be available in electronic books. For more information about Wiley products, visit our web site at www.wiley.com.

Library of Congress Cataloging-in-Publication Data:
Stull, Craig.
  Tuned in: uncover the extraordinary opportunities that lead to business breakthroughs/ Craig Stull, Phil Myers, and David Meerman Scott.
      p. cm.
  Includes bibliographical references and index.
  ISBN 978-0-470-26036-4 (cloth)
  1. Success in business. 2. Creative ability in business. I. Myers, Phil.
II. Scott, David Meerman. III. Title.

  HF5386.S886 2008
  658.4'09–dc22

                                                                2007051634

Printed in the United States of America
10 9 8 7 6 5 4 3 2

For the Tuned In Leaders in Our Lives

The women who inspired us—our wives Karen, Diane,
and Yukari—and the fabulous team and community
of customers we have at Pragmatic Marketing,
the people who remind us every day how valuable
this concept is.

Contents

1

Why Didn't We Think of That?

Products and services that resonate

The Japanese salaryman works notoriously long hours. He's in the office until 9 or 10 p.m. and sometimes goes out for drinks and maybe some karaoke singing with colleagues after that. But there's a problem. In the big cities like Tokyo, Osaka, and Nagoya, the last train leaves for the suburbs around midnight. So, as the result of a long day at the office and perhaps a few beers, when a Japanese office worker gets on that last train, he often falls asleep.[1]

Sometimes he misses his stop.

When the train pulls into the station at the end of the line, the conductors pass through the cars and find a surprising number of sleeping salarymen. They do what's necessary to wake up the wage warriors and push them out the train door. The dazed salarymen then make their way into the quiet night—briefcases in hand, neckties askew—and find themselves in a rice-growing country town many miles from the city. They're also far from their home stops, which passed by an hour before (perhaps as they were dreaming of that perfect rendition of "Take Me Home, Country Roads" at the karaoke bar).

Next train home? Not 'til first thing in the morning, still three or four hours away. A taxi? Several hundred bucks. Instead, our accidental travelers notice a hotel just across the street! And there are vacancies!

And so the blue-suited businessmen head toward their unexpected deliverance. When they arrive at the hotel, they're greeted and perhaps handed a toilet kit with toothbrush and razor. Best of all, they'll pay far less than they would have for taxi fare. A place to sleep until morning . . . problem solved.

Who would have thought to build a hotel at the end of a train line, far from anywhere important? Well, smart Japanese hotel owners tuned in to a previously ignored market problem that a well-placed hotel could fix. They identified a particular buyer of hotel services (the overworked and exhausted salaryman), and they've built growing, profitable businesses around that niche—in the least likely places, like lonely towns many miles from the nearest big city. (Similar inns, such as Wellbe Hotels in Nagoya, have sprung up near stations in busy business centers and cater to those who miss that last train completely.)[2]

We're fascinated with success stories like these—buyer experiences that resonate because they perfectly address market problems that people are prepared to pay money to solve. We've identified the patterns of success (and failure), and in these pages we'll introduce you to dozens of products and services that resonate with their markets. We'll also tell you about some that don't, and we'll explain why not. Most importantly, we'll teach you the Tuned In Process so you can replicate the winners' success in your own organization.

Tuned In shows you how to find overlooked marketplace problems that, if solved, bring in customers who willingly buy your products and services without being coerced.

Tuned In—The Process and the Book

In these pages we will share the Tuned In Process, a six-step method for creating a *resonator*: a product or service that so perfectly solves problems for buyers that it sells itself. Starbucks, *American Idol,* and

Google are resonators. Were these products and services created by people smarter, luckier, or born with more talent than the rest of us? *No*. We'll show you that real success in the marketplace is not based on creativity or clever marketing. Anyone can create products and services that resonate. All you need to do is stop *guessing* what people need and start spending your time building real and deep connections to what your buyers value most. We'll show you how to apply the Tuned In Process to find unsolved problems in your marketplace and how you can create breakthrough experiences that people are eager to spend money on.

As we introduce the Tuned In Process, we'll use dozens of examples of companies that have tuned into their market and created resonators. We've studied the introduction of thousands of products, including those from large, well-known companies like Ford Motor Company, Microsoft, and GE; breakout bestsellers from Apple, Red Bull, and Google; and niche offerings from players you may have never heard of like National Community Church, GoPro, and Zipcar.

Any organization—companies large and small, nonprofits, government agencies, entrepreneurs and independent professionals, even churches, authors, and rock bands—can benefit from getting tuned in, because they'll start to create the products and services that people want to buy.

Why Listen to Us?

In the middle of 2006, the three of us came together to talk about the ideas that came to be this book. Many of our clients had told us that they wanted an overview of the process we teach, but in an easy-to-digest package they could share with others. We realized that we had discovered a market problem—a need for a book like this one—and that we had the knowledge (rooted in years of teaching the Tuned In Process) to solve it. Thus, we hope this project will help these ideas get to people in many more industries, job functions, and countries than we reach today through our live speeches and in-person seminars.

As we've come together to write this book, we've drawn from our personal strengths. As founder and CEO of Pragmatic Marketing, Craig's methodologies have been taught to over 45,000 executives, product managers, and marketing people at over 3,000 companies. Phil has been a CEO or senior manager at three start-ups that grew into market leaders, with two leading to successful initial public offerings. David is an expert in *The New Rules of Marketing & PR* (the title of his most recent bestselling book), bringing a deep understanding of how to reach buyers directly using social media, and with an eye toward helping customers solve their problems.[3]

In the next chapter, "Tuned Out . . . and Just Guessing," we'll debunk three common myths about what leads to success. Although it may be surprising to many people, we've learned that: (1) relying on innovation isn't the answer, (2) focusing on revenue often leads to failure, and (3) listening to your customers creates dangerous false signals. We'll show you why. Armed with this understanding, you will eliminate the struggle to make connections with your marketplace. Chapter 3 will ground you in the Tuned In Process so you understand how to apply it to build, market, and sell what your buyers want to purchase.

The Tuned In Process includes six steps, and each is explored further in its own detailed chapter so you can apply its lessons to your business:

 Step 1: Find Unresolved Problems—How do we know what market and product to focus on?

Step 2: Understand Buyer Personas—How do we identify who will buy our offering?

 Step 3: Quantify the Impact—How do we know if we have a potential winner?

Step 4: Create Breakthrough Experiences—How do we build a competitive advantage?

Step 5: Articulate Powerful Ideas—How do we establish memorable concepts that speak to the problems buyers have?

Step 6: Establish Authentic Connections—How do we tell our buyers that we've solved their problems so they buy from us?

The crowning touch to the Tuned In Process is the creation of a resonator, a product or service that buyers want to talk about, buy, and recommend. In the remaining chapters, we'll explore what it takes to transform your organization by cultivating a tuned in culture and how to become and remain a market leader. To make it easy for you to skim parts of the book and to refer back as you're reading, we've included chapter summaries at the end of each chapter.

What's fascinating about the tuned in approach is that it works amazingly well for all kinds of organizations. We've identified nonprofits, business-to-business enterprises, e-commerce companies, independent consultants, churches, and even dentists and lawyers who have created resonators and built growing and profitable businesses. Although they serve a wide variety of markets, these different types of organizations all have the same potential to discover resonators. By being tuned in, they can listen intently, embrace buyer needs passionately, and work diligently to create the best possible customer experience.

Without further ado, we'd like to introduce you to our first tuned in businessperson. If his story doesn't speak to you, never fear; you'll meet dozens more.

The Realtor Who Resonates

In our experience, real estate agents lack much in the way of distinguishing characteristics. Get past the business card or the kind of car the agent uses to ferry clients, and realtors seem interchangeable, don't they? When you go to list a home, a realtor says, "Sign here. We take 6 percent commission, and I'll need an exclusive agreement. . . . By the way, how soon can you have the house clean so I can show it?" And like most salespeople, many realtors immediately talk discounting. "What's the lowest price you would sell the home for?" they ask. By being insular and not understanding the true problems faced by people who want to sell their homes, the typical real estate agent focuses on the wrong things.

We've often mused about how much more successful realtors would be if they tuned in to their marketplaces. What if a realtor spent time understanding market problems first? Could he or she then build a breakthrough product experience *in what most people say is a commodity business?* After all, real-estate listing services are all pretty much the same, right? What if this renegade agent also used the Tuned In Process to establish authentic connections with buyers—would the agent earn more business as a result? Could real estate services resonate and create a platform to build a thriving and profitable business? Could someone break out of the pack?

Well, we have our answer, or rather our agent. His name is Russell Shaw and he has been a realtor in the Phoenix area for thirty years.[4] Shaw is associated with a realty firm, but that's where his similarity with other realtors ends. He approaches building and marketing his services by being tuned in. Shaw built his business, the Russell Shaw Group, by first understanding the problems that sellers face:

+ "I want my home to sell *fast.*"
+ "I want to *get as much money* for my house as I can."
+ "I would like to *avoid realtor's commissions* if I can, but I hesitate to try selling my home myself because of the risks involved."
+ "If my realtor is not meeting my expectations, I *don't want to be stuck with a long-term contract.*"

Shaw's breakthrough product experience is the "No Hassle List-ing." Using Shaw's service, sellers list with him for a reasonable 4 per-cent fee but still have the option to sell their home themselves and owe him nothing (although they may still use the Russell Shaw Group to help with the escrow work for a 1 percent fee if they wish).

"Our objectives are to get you the most money in the least time, and with the fewest hassles," Shaw says. "We want to provide the best service in the industry. Period. We want to make you so satisfied that you listed your home with us that you will gladly refer us to your friends."

Shaw articulates his idea by stating that he is "applying for a job" with you. If you aren't happy with the job he does, you can fire him at any time with no obligations or costly consequences. But odds are that you will be happy, because the average home listed with the Russell Shaw Group, even during the slow 2007 housing market, sells in less than forty-five days (versus 111 days for other realtors in the area), and most of Shaw's listings sell for the full price. If you've ever sold a home, you'll likely agree with us that this idea is a resonator.

Shaw spent two years identifying and refining his ideas about which problems resonate with home sellers. He tuned in. Shaw even gives potential clients a list of fourteen questions to ask his compet-itors, questions that show the No Hassle Listing system is in a class by itself. Shaw generates so much business from it that he requires a support staff of sixteen people, including six listing/buying special-ists, two transaction managers, seven administrators, and even a marketing manager!

Finally, a realtor who understands the problems sellers face and has a solution for them! While the average realtor sells eight to twelve homes a year, and "top" realtors sell twenty-two to thirty homes a year, Shaw sold a remarkable 370 homes in 2007.

"Many agents think their most important job is satisfying the customer," Shaw says. "I don't think that's true. I believe that satis-fying the customer is simply the minimum requirement for staying in business. My staff and I work constantly to improve our systems, processes, and services to go well beyond the standard level of 'ser-vice' provided by most agents."

Would you recommend *your* realtor to your friends?

We're convinced that if tuned in people like Shaw can build a resonator in a crowded and long-established market like real estate, you can too. And the Tuned In Process will show you how.

Getting Tuned In

How hard is it to get connected to a market and create a product or service that people want to buy? Based on our decades of experience working with thousands of companies, we're here to tell you that *getting tuned in is not difficult.* But creating a resonator does require a new way of thinking about how you build products and services and how you introduce them to the marketplace. Most organizations are *tuned out.* In fact, we see all kinds of organizations make the same common mistakes again and again.

Here are a few common mistakes that cause products and services to fail:

+ **Guessing**—Assuming *company insiders* know more than buyers about what they want to buy
+ **Assuming**—Basing products and services on what *current customers* request rather than on an understanding of unsolved problems that other people will pay money to fix
+ **Telling**—Trying to *create a need* in the market by relying on expensive advertising or an army of salespeople

We've developed the Tuned In Process to allow companies to create success again and again. We see these same principles at work in a wide range of successful product experiences, like business-to-business technology products, fast-food chains, and professional services firms. We know for certain that if you apply the six-step Tuned In Process to your own business (no matter what you sell), you will have a much better chance at success.

The Resonator

"1,000 Songs in Your Pocket"[5]
"When It Absolutely, Positively Has to Be There Overnight"[6]

The process for replicating success starts with getting tuned in to potential customers. Understanding your market and your buyers through in-depth interviewing is by far the most effective way to discover *unresolved market problems* that people will pay money to solve. Meeting with potential buyers on their own turf (in their homes or workplaces, or even on the street) is the starting point for identifying a resonator: a breakthrough product or service that buyers immediately understand has value to them, even if they have never heard of your company or its products before. The iPod is a resonator. When it launched, FedEx was a huge resonator, and it still is.

The Anatomy of a Resonator:

+ *The perfect solution to a specific problem*
+ *A product or service that people want to buy without being coerced*
+ *An offering that establishes a real and direct connection to what your market values most*
+ *An idea that people immediately understand has value to them, even if they have never heard of your company or its products and services*

When you see a powerful, smartly articulated idea for a product or service that solves a problem for you, such as the iPod ("1,000 Songs in Your Pocket") or FedEx ("When It Absolutely, Positively Has to Be There Overnight"), you immediately grasp its meaning. *It resonates.* These words aren't mere taglines or slogans dreamed up by an agency and peddled with expensive advertising. You can learn to systematically develop powerful ideas like these by studying the Tuned In Process.

Tuned in organizations are much more likely to create resonators. The culture of tuned in companies incorporates focused, "outside-in" thinking, instead of the typical inside-out orientation. In other words, the tuned in company constantly listens to, observes, and understands the problems that buyers are willing to pay money to solve instead of holding endless meetings of company insiders all trying to guess what people want. The tuned in organization is always looking for more opportunities to create resonators.

The Tuned In Organization

 The most successful organizations get tuned in to their markets; we'll introduce you to dozens of them. Leaders at these companies largely ignore the competition. Instead, they focus their energies on the problems that buyers are

willing to spend money to solve. The concept applies to any business, product, or service:[7]

+ *Tuned in companies*—large and small, established and upstart—resonate when they create products people want to buy. Nintendo's Wii revolutionized the gaming industry when it created a fun, simple, interactive experience that enabled groups of friends and families to play virtual sports, action, and war games without any previous experience with video games.
+ The *tuned in entrepreneur* solves real problems in the market rather than creating some widget because he thinks it's cool. Richard Branson, a serial entrepreneur, has developed 350 companies over a thirty-year career through his Virgin brands, each aligned to solve a discrete market problem that he and his team identified.
+ The *tuned in professional services firm* (lawyers, doctors, accountants) doesn't just create a "me too" practice and stick the same old advertisement in the yellow pages. Instead, these firms leverage the new rules of marketing to build an online audience. Search for anything related to Kansas and family law and you'll find Grant D. Griffiths at the top of the list. Griffiths takes a thought leadership approach to marketing his firm, and he consequently makes connections that bring him several new potential customers a week . . . free.
+ The *tuned in nonprofit* understands people's motivation for contributing money and time to a cause. Habitat for Humanity has experienced more than a decade of consistent growth in donations of time and money, due in large part to its creative strategies for partnering with local community, church, youth, and government organizations. Habitat for Humanity has built more than 200,000 homes.
+ The *tuned in politician* understands voter problems and the reasons why people vote for a particular candidate. Barack Obama's campaign raised more than $102 million in its initial phases (through the end of 2007) second among all U.S. presidential candidates). His platform centered around powerful ideas, "the Audacity of Hope" and "change," has attracted more than one million contributors to his

campaign, a strong indicator of a grass roots movement. At this writing, the primary season is just starting, and Obama is not the front-runner. But his upstart candidacy clearly resonates with many voters.

✦ The *tuned in church* connects to people's spiritual and emotional needs with services that resonate across traditional and nontraditional mediums. Joel Osteen now counts more than 42,000 weekly attendees at his services, and millions more through his TV and online communications. His book, *Your Best Life Now*, has sold more than 2.5 million copies.

✦ The *tuned in entertainer, rock band, or motivational speaker* understands the tastes or needs of his potential audience. Jon Stewart tuned in to young TV watchers and brought a life-saving expansion in viewership to a fake news show that had been a cult favorite on a little-known cable channel. Since Jon Stewart took over *The Daily Show* in 1999, its ratings have soared among young adults in its time slot.

✦ We'd argue that *tuned in jobseekers* create a better picture of themselves as candidates for employment when they go easy on embellishing their credentials and talk more about solving an employer's problems.

Is *Tuned In* for You?

At this point, we suspect that you're saying to yourself something like "hey that's obvious" or "it sounds easy." We frequently hear these sorts of reactions when we present these ideas live in our speeches and seminars. If that's what you're thinking, you're right! One of the beautiful things about getting tuned in is that it's easy to understand how to do it. In fact, many successful business leaders had been applying these principles successfully long before we began teaching the process or writing it down in this book.

But hold on!

You're probably also thinking this: "If it's so easy to understand and it makes so much sense, why don't more companies get tuned in?" As it turns out, numerous organizational pitfalls can get in the way. We meet with companies all the time whose executives struggle to answer some very basic questions:

+ What business are we in?
+ What businesses are we *not* in?
+ Who are our buyers?
+ What's unique about our offering?
+ What's our positioning strategy?
+ How can we compete?
+ Why do the other guys seem to win more often?
+ How can we turn a profit?

When we hit these walls with business leaders, we ask ourselves why. How could they not have good answers to these fundamental questions? What we've come to realize is that most business professionals just aren't tuned in.

> **Rather than focusing on buyers and their problems, the organizations that struggle to resonate in their marketplace are the ones that develop offerings using inside-out thinking.**

Instead of going out into the marketplace to try to understand people's problems and then bringing this information back to the company, tuned out companies try to develop products exclusively within their own walls, based entirely on what they already know. Then they try all sorts of gimmicks and buy expensive advertising to take the dissonant ideas out into the market. This inside-out approach (what we call being tuned out) is much more likely to lead to failure—and to struggles with questions like those above.

What Led to *Tuned In*?

Tuned In is not a book on a new business theory. Instead, it's a proven process for building and sustaining success. When we came together to write this book, we drew upon our collective experience running companies. A critical input to the book has been the understanding that we've developed at Pragmatic Marketing through having trained 45,000 executives, product managers, and marketing people at over 3,000 companies in the Tuned In Process.

But we wanted to dig deeper to validate independent research telling us that market-driven companies were 31 percent more profitable, spent twice as much on research as they did on development, and had 20 percent higher customer satisfaction rates.[8] So we tapped into our own research data from thousands of people within companies large and small that Pragmatic Marketing has surveyed each year since 2000.[9] The surveys look at how executives, marketing specialists, and product management professionals make key product decisions and what parts of the marketing mix are most effective. We also conducted detailed interviews of nearly one hundred CEOs and founders of companies to learn how they started their businesses, how they operate today, and why some of their products and services fail while others succeed.

We want to thank the hundreds of entrepreneurs, business executives, managers of nonprofits, professional services providers, and leaders of other organizations for their help in developing the ideas in this book. They gave us the inspiration and the road map for how organizations get tuned in, and you'll meet many of them in these pages.

A note on terms: Throughout the book, when we use the word "company" and "organization" we're including all types of organizations and individuals. Feel free to insert "nonprofit," "government agency," "political candidate," "church," "school," "sports team," "professional service person," or other entity in place of "company" and "organization" in your mind. Similarly, we use the word "buyers," which also means "subscribers," "voters," "volunteers," "applicants," and "donors." Are you an independent professional—a lawyer, accountant, or real estate agent? The need to get tuned in applies to you just as much as to a corporation. Ditto for nonprofits focused on increasing donations and volunteers, political campaigns looking for votes, schools that want to increase application numbers, consultants searching for business, and churches seeking new members.

In the next chapter, we'll take a look at some of the ways that typical organizational structures cause companies to be tuned out. Chapter 3 is an introduction to the Tuned In Process, while

Chapters 4 through 9 take detailed looks at each of the six steps in the Tuned In Process. Best of all, throughout the book we'll offer interesting examples of diverse organizations (like the Russell Shaw Group) that have gotten tuned in to their markets; we hope you'll enjoy learning from their tremendous success.

Chapter Summary

+ Why do some products and services fail while others succeed? That question keeps many CEOs, venture capitalists, nonprofit executives, entrepreneurs, employees, and shareholders up at night.

+ The culture of tuned in companies incorporates focused "outside-in" thinking instead of the typical inside-out orientation. In other words, the tuned in company constantly listens, observes, and understands the problems that buyers are willing to pay money to solve instead of participating in endless meetings of company insiders all trying to guess what people want.

+ But the process of becoming *tuned in* does require a new way of thinking about how you build products and services and how you introduce them to the marketplace.

+ Meeting with people on their own turf (in their homes or workplaces, or even on the street) is the starting point to identify what we call a *resonator:* a breakthrough product or service that buyers immediately understand has value to them, even if they have never heard of your company or its products before.

+ Understanding your market and your buyers through in-depth interviewing is by far the most effective way to discover unresolved market problems that people will pay money to solve.

+ The necessary steps for discovering, creating, and launching a resonator are not difficult. But they do require that you do things differently than you're probably doing them today.

+ Organizations make the same common mistakes again and again: guessing at what the market wants, basing products and services on what *current customers* request, and trying to *create a need* in the market by relying on expensive advertising or an army of salespeople.

2

Tuned Out . . . and Just Guessing

Eliminate the struggle to make connections with your marketplace

In the movie *Big*, a young boy named Josh makes a wish at a fair-ground machine. Josh wants to be "big," and when he wakes up the following morning his wish has been granted. Josh now dwells in a grown-up body (played brilliantly by Tom Hanks), but he is still the same twelve-year-old kid inside. In his new body, Josh must learn how to cope with the unfamiliar world of grownup relationships, including with his coworkers at a toy company. Josh is great at his new job because, as a real twelve-year-old inside, he is absolutely *tuned in* to what children want to play with.

Josh's encounters with the tuned out grown-ups are revealing. They are exactly the sorts of discussions we know from experience happen inside most companies:

> PAUL: (one of Josh's coworkers): These tests were conducted over a six-month period using a double-blind format of eight

overlapping demographic groups. Every region of the country was sampled. The focus testing showed a solid base in the nine- to eleven-year-old bracket, with a possible carryover into the twelve-year-olds. When you consider that Nobots and Transformers pull over 37 percent market share, and that we are targeting the same area, I think that we should see one-quarter of that and that is one-fifth of the total revenue from all of last year. Any questions? Yes? Yes?

JOSH: I don't get it.

PAUL: What exactly don't you get?

JOSH: It turns from a building into a robot, right?

PAUL: Precisely.

JOSH: Well, what's fun about that?

PAUL: Well, if you had read your industry breakdown, you would see that our success in the action figure area has climbed from 27 percent to 45 percent in the last two years. There, that might help.

JOSH: Oh.

PAUL: Yes?

JOSH: I still don't get it.

We meet employees like Paul all the time, corporate types who dream up a product based on gut feel and then use data (in this case, focus groups and sales figures for related products) to make him and his colleagues believe his product is a winner. But it is clear from Josh's reaction that nobody actually listened to kids to find out what they might think is fun to play with. If you're in the toy business, your job is to find out how to help kids have fun.

In fact, Josh's opinion alone isn't enough. His company should still get out of the office and go interview other children. Interviewing buyers on their home turf reveals much more about how to develop a product than does merely showing them an "inside-out" product in a focus group.

But We're the Experts!

Of all the causes of tuned out behavior, the most common we've observed is the logical (but incorrect) assumption that, because you're an expert in a market or industry, you therefore know more than your buyers about how your product can solve their problems. It's natural, for instance, for twenty-year auto industry veterans to assume they know more than a hundred mothers do about how to drive preschool-age children around town each day. Too often, this kind of assumption results in poor products, such as those created when Detroit product development experts just design the radio (or keyless entry system, or cupholder layout) that they themselves would want to buy.

When was the last time you bought your company's product?

In the late 1960s, Woodstream Corporation, announced that it had built a better mousetrap.[1] With great fanfare, the company launched the new product into the marketplace, claiming that it was even better than their wooden, spring-based Victor mousetrap, a classic that had sold more than a *billion* units since the company introduced it in 1890. Alas, the world did not beat a second path to the company's door. The new, "better" mousetrap was a flop, and the company had to revert back to its "old-fashioned" wooden model. A company spokesperson said, "We should have spent more time researching housewives, and less time researching mice." Today, the product that people want to buy—the Victor mousetrap—is still the most recognized brand name in rodent control.

Executives, product development people, and marketers all want to believe that they've got all the answers. They're like the guys at Woodstream Corporation who thought that they could make a better mousetrap because they were the experts. The entrepreneur wants to go with her gut. The product manager wants to recreate a past success. The marketer wants to rely on expensive advertising to buy market share, or to gamble on a huge *Time* magazine, *Wall Street Journal,* or *Today Show* media hit. But these seat-of-your-pants approaches involve much more *risk.* Going on intuition, buying your way in with expensive advertising, or begging your way in by hoping for media coverage simply does not work as often or as well as being tuned in.

The Dollar Nobody Wanted

In 1979, the U.S. government introduced the Susan B. Anthony dollar coin.[2] We can imagine the thought process inside the United States Mint: "For our next product, we'll create an exciting new currency option that will cost us less than paper dollars because each one will last longer. And we can honor an American feminist leader at the same time!" This is a classic case of tuned out product development. Instead of solving a *buyer* problem, the Susan B. Anthony dollar was designed to solve a problem that faced *the organization that created it*: the United States Mint.

The coin was universally rejected within the first ninety days because it didn't solve any significant existing problems for consumers. On the other hand, it did introduce new problems. In particular, the dollar coin was remarkably similar to the quarter in size and color, confusing the people who used it and making it less likely that they'd want to use it in the future.

Didn't anyone test the coin with consumers? Actually, the government had indeed contracted with a market research firm before developing the Susan B. Anthony dollar. We are told that extensive consumer research indicated the coin would be a miserable failure. However, government officials tuned out, ignored the data, and charged forward because the vending machine lobby convinced the government that America needed a dollar coin. And since the vending machines in operation at the time couldn't, without extensive retooling, accept coins that were significantly larger or different than a quarter, they insisted on the silly size that was so similar to a quarter. The original design called for a hendecagon-shaped edge to the coin, but the vending machine manufacturers protested the 11-sided option. In the end nobody (except for coin collectors) wanted it, so at the end of production, the United States Department of the Treasury was left with hundreds of millions of unused coins in its vaults.

If We're Not Tuned In, What Are We?

As we've analyzed hundreds of companies to understand the process of becoming (and staying) tuned in, we've determined that most have a single dominant focus that drives their approach to business. Think of it as a "company personality" that determines how an organization structures itself and behaves in the market. The most successful organizations are tuned in. Whenever leaders create products or services—for potential new customers or even entirely new markets—they seek to solve buyer problems first.

However, we have identified three other common organizational cultures. When an organization allows one of these three cultures to dominate, the resulting approach to business is very different from the one we outline in the Tuned In Process:

+ Innovation Is Everything
+ Revenue Cures All
+ Customers Know Best

While most tuned out companies exhibit at least a small amount of each of these driving behaviors, one usually dominates. And the choice directly correlates to their success (or failure). Let's explore each of these in further detail.

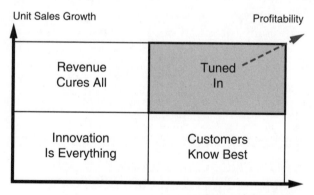

Tuned in businesses perform better than companies driven by innovation, revenue growth, or customer satisfaction—without sacrificing the benefits of any of these three cultures.

Debunking the Myth That "Innovation Is Everything"

These days innovation is hot. Check out all the magazine articles, business school courses, and books on the subject and you'll find countless examples detailing how innovation creates break-throughs. This has led many organizations (start-ups in particular) to focus exclusively on their ability to innovate and to create a disruptive breakthrough that will make them famous. But directionless innovation is a common road to the business scrap heap.

The culture of "Innovation Is Everything" breeds tuned out behaviors. Innovation-driven leaders tend to listen only to themselves, although they do track competitors religiously. These companies fixate on "one-upping" alternative products in the marketplace. And they obsess about who's getting credit for the most clever or unique inventions.

Focusing on "changing the game" is not inherently a bad thing. Some organizations are really good at creating and marketing innovative products—Bose, Nike, and Brookstone are three that come to mind. Unfortunately, what we tend to see more often are companies that *innovate for innovation's sake*, using inside-out thinking. In other words, they create products that are new, hip, and cool or have new, never-before-seen features. But these feature-laden products and services aren't developed in response to buyer-defined needs. While it is *possible* that a product or service created by a tuned out, innovation-driven company will catch on, it is much less likely than if the innovation were specifically designed to solve market problems. As a result, these innovation-led companies invest big resources in hopes of a big win (much like a baseball player swinging for a home run on each pitch). Their risk of failure is huge.

Only when an innovation solves people's problems does it become a potent force.

We realize we're being a bit radical here. But consider the piles of money plowed into innovation during the dot-com boom.

Venture capital firms funded innovative e-commerce companies, innovative Web tool developers, and innovative portal sites that sounded new, hip, and, well . . . innovative. Anything with an "e" in front of it qualified. But unless they solved an underlying problem, most of these exciting innovations have become distant memories. Remember: the truly successful Web companies, such as eBay, Yahoo, and Amazon, solved market problems.

We've also noticed that many innovation-driven companies obsess over competitors' moves and try to make incremental (and innovative!) improvements to what the other guys are doing. This approach assumes that your competitors are already connected to the things your market values most and that the game is just a simple matter of establishing a clear area of superiority (through innovation, of course). Another problem with this approach is that you tend to create products and services that are "better" than the other guy's because they are bigger, smaller, faster, or cheaper. Too often, your customers just don't care. Focusing on your competitors is a tit-for-tat game that rarely produces a market leader.

However, there's an important distinction to be made here. It is possible for a tuned in organization to learn about an unresolved market problem connected to another company's product. For example, buyer interviews might reveal that people are ready to pay money for a product that they describe in terms of the competitor's product ("a good-quality haircut in half the time that I would need to spend at the hairdresser in town"). Creating a product to solve this problem is definitely an example of tuned in behavior, even though the market problem is expressed as a comparison with an existing product.

But, in the end, a corporate personality built around innovation by itself has a low probability of success. Obsessing over the competition's product, or over your own product's increased performance or new features, means you aren't focused on the most important success driver: the market problems faced by your buyers. And, believe us, there is no such thing as the creative dreamer, sitting in an isolated office, who builds products that succeed every time. The dreams may sometimes hit a chord, but the vast majority of products made by innovation-driven companies just don't resonate with the market.

Debunking the Myth That "Revenue Cures All"

A second culture and strategy we see often is founded on the belief that revenue and sales are always the most important goals. This culture often emerges soon after an initial round of fund-raising or some other infusion of capital. When companies enter a perceived growth phase (dictated by the strength of a market opportunity or some early wins), it is common for outsiders (such as investors, the board of directors, or your spouse) to insist on a strong sales focus. In larger organizations, a highly charged sales executive is often hired; some companies even make the new salesperson the president and/or COO.

"Getting serious about sales" sometimes results in an initial brief period of success resulting from sheer force of will to push solutions into the market. But because the revenue-driven company will often lower its prices and cut corners as it hunts business—signing any contract to make the numbers and telling any story to close the sale—it's not long before the organization becomes tuned out to the real market problems of buyers. Then the salespeople start making promises that the company can't afford to keep. Non–revenue-generating departments (such as marketing, customer service, and product development) often suffer from reduced influence and resources. The company may even end up acquiring other companies and products to support the dynamic requests of sales, often resulting in duplicate offerings and lengthy integration programs that drive up costs without improving growth or customer satisfaction.

> **The revenue-driven organization worries about individual sales opportunities one at a time, rather than what resonates with a large marketplace.**

In many consumer products the "Revenue Cures All" approach results in jumping on the hype cycle. Some organizations spend huge amounts of money on expensive advertising in attempts to buy their way into buyers' minds. These tuned out organizations believe that TV commercials, direct mail, and other forms of interruption-based marketing are the tools they need to succeed. Instead of spending time understanding buyers and their problems, hype-driven companies spend time with their agencies working on campaigns to bombard people with slogans and messages. We're not against advertising when used as a strategy to communicate powerful ideas that already resonate with people. The "Where's the Beef" campaign from Wendy's worked because it communicated an answer to buyers' problems.[3] (Hamburgers had beef patties that were too small.) But the hype-driven company *manufactures* buzz that has very little to do with helping people solve problems.

Debunking the Myth That "Customers Know Best"

There are thousands of books, countless blogs and forums, hundreds of conferences, and lots of plain old common sense that suggest an unrelenting focus on the *customer* is the best way to guide an organization. But there is a fundamental flaw with being a customer-driven organization: Your existing customers represent a small percentage of your opportunity, they have different market problems than noncustomers (buyers who don't yet do business with you), and—most importantly—they only frame their view of your future based on incremental improvements to their *past* experiences.

For example, if a company in the late 1990s that made and sold portable music devices asked their existing customers what they wanted, they might say "more storage" or a "smaller unit." The companies that listened to their customers all missed the biggest market problems that were identified by Apple when they developed the iPod: the existing portable devices were too difficult to use and impractical for downloading and managing more than a few songs.

> **Because the customer-driven organization relies on existing customer requests for endless extensions to existing product lines, the company can't develop breakthrough products and services that resonate with noncustomers.**

Don't misunderstand us—we're all in favor of great customer service. We just don't believe that an obsession focused solely on your *existing* customers is the right way to design and build product experiences and to reach the *total* market. Eventually, the customer-driven company gets bogged down by taking baby steps to tweak features in existing offerings (to please existing customers) rather than making the bold leap to develop new products and services that solve potential buyers' problems.

Assuming that your customer knows best is a comfortable strategy, because it's very easy to get feedback about how to conduct your business. "What do you want us to create next?" you ask. The customer is delighted to tell you. But you have listened to only a *few* people (those you already do business with) rather than *many* (the untapped market). Unfortunately, working only for your existing customers usually results in sleepy, increasingly unprofitable companies.

A Missionary Sell?

Ultimately, a focus solely on any of these approaches—being a customer-, revenue-, or innovation-driven company—*is more risky*. It is possible to build success, but the odds are stacked against you. And if you do beat the odds and develop a winner, you may still fail later. It might take years for the results of being tuned out to become apparent if your initially successful product can be turned into a cash cow.

Resonators are in the market, not in your mind.

We often see tuned out companies create products and services that do not resonate. To compensate, they must adopt drastic strategies to drum up business for their offerings. You know how many companies talk about their "product evangelists"? And how many organizations say that they are "missionaries in the market" and that they need to "educate people about the issues so that they see the value of our product or service"? These missionary selling strategies are simply symptoms of a tuned out company. You shouldn't have to wave your arms around and shout at people to convince them to pay attention to your product or service.

A resonator is a product or service that sells itself.

The tuned in, market-driven company understands market problems and builds products that resonate; these practices drive both sales and customer satisfaction.

Are You Tuned In or Tuned Out?

If your organizational culture is closest to one of the three that we've outlined above, it means your organization is tuned out. The key distinction is that being tuned out requires that you *guess* when making important decisions such as what product to build, who to try to sell it to, where to sell it, and so on. But each time you guess at one of these elements, you introduce more risk into your business.

Consider your own organization. How would you answer these questions?

- ✦ Do you build products based on what company insiders feel is best?
- ✦ Do you use advertising campaigns to "create the need" in the market?
- ✦ Do the salespeople dictate what goes into new products?
- ✦ Do you watch the competition and make moves to follow them?
- ✦ Do you only sell (and improve upon) whatever products you already have on the shelf?
- ✦ Is the founder's (or CEO's) opinion the most important?
- ✦ Are major decisions based on financial data alone?
- ✦ Is gaining market share your primary objective?

You probably realize that a "yes" answer to *any* of these questions means you've got some of the symptoms of being tuned out and that you're guessing at what your market requires.

Resisting the Gravitational Force

So why are people tuned out? Why are they guessing? If we look closely enough, we find a rather simple explanation. While it's not difficult to understand how to get tuned in, actually implementing the Tuned In Process is outside of many people's comfort zone.

While it's not difficult to understand how to get tuned in and transform your business, it's just easier to tune out.

We often lament what we've termed the "gravitational force" that tends to pull companies back to a normal state of being tuned out. Think about your organization's internal meetings for a moment. When you and your colleagues are in a conference room talking about how to create a product, market it, communicate with your buyers about it, or launch it into the market, how often do you make decisions based on mere guesswork? How often do you rely on experience and gut feel instead of the information you've collected from buyers who have a problem that your product or service solves? How often do you assume that the competition knows something important that you don't and that you should just copy them willy-nilly? How often do you participate in internal meetings to discuss "strategy" or "positioning" or "messaging," and then the entire discussion is based on the opinions of the people in the room and not the facts? How often does the person with the loudest voice in your conference room (or the executive with the biggest title) win an argument? Or consider this: how often are your organization's internal problems (to get a product to market, reduce costs, or impress the board and shareholders) more urgent to you than your buyers' problems?

A colleague of ours was recently helping plan a retreat for a university group. During a typical steering committee meeting, the group decided that an on-campus site was best because (they thought) there would be a bigger perceived time commitment involved in traveling to an off-campus retreat site. One night over dinner, our colleague mentioned the idea to a few new members (the "buyers" that the university group hopes will stick around and become active members) before finalizing the plans. It turns out that he and the rest of the committee were wrong—the new members actually *wanted* the event held off campus. Why? Because they're all freshmen who live in the dorms and don't have cars, so they wanted a chance to get off campus and see more of the surrounding area. Our colleague admitted that he and the committee were thinking, at least in part, about their own problems, not those of their buyers.

"Your opinion, although interesting, is irrelevant."

We've got a simple saying that we use again and again when meetings and discussions fall victim to the inevitable gravitational force that draws groups away from the Tuned In Process that we know works: *your opinion, although interesting, is irrelevant.* We use the phrase to emphasize these ideas in our seminars and speeches, and we use it when we meet with one another. At tuned in companies, the boss's opinion, although interesting, is irrelevant; the founder's opinion, although interesting, is irrelevant; the salesperson's opinion, although interesting, is irrelevant. Most importantly, *your* opinion, although interesting, is irrelevant. *What matters is your buyers' opinions.* What market problems can your company solve with its products and services? Have you interviewed buyers, and do you understand their problems in detail?

We've participated in countless internal meetings that devolve into the usual tuned out nonsense—wild speculation about what new product or service might get the company out of the third-place position in the market or what slick advertising campaign will juice the sales results enough to appease the stockholders. These sessions *always* end in a guessing game about market needs; none of the opinions are ever grounded in hard data obtained by speaking to buyers about their problems.

But we've also been in meetings where one person, perhaps a product manager or marketing manager (or in the case of a much smaller organization, maybe it's the entrepreneurial owner's spouse), says something like this: "Well I've interviewed twenty potential customers, and here's what I've learned . . ."

Holy cow!

The room goes silent. Everybody leans forward. The BS artists clam up. Somebody has data! *We can stop guessing!*

We know that staying tuned in is difficult, particularly at first. You try your best to make decisions based on the market, but it's hard to do so consistently. The gravitational force pulls you back to relying on your own opinion in much the same way that poor eating and exercise habits creep back into the lifestyle of many people who are working to stay fit and healthy. We're certain that every company, even those we consider role models for the Tuned In Process, have slipped into relying on gut feel and instinct from time to time. Hey, we've done it too! As we were meeting to discuss marketing and promotional decisions for this book—things like potential book titles, and the best way to get the book into the marketplace—we fell into the behavior we advise others to avoid. One of us would passionately argue some point (a favorite subtitle perhaps) by using the words, "I think . . . " Then the other two would respond, mercilessly, with "*Your opinion, although interesting, is irrelevant.*"

Organizations that develop products without first understanding market problems and buyer personas introduce a significant element of risk to their businesses. Sure, in some cases you can come up with a breakthrough all on your own and create some level of market success. It is *possible*. But, it's more likely that you'll miss the key to success that lies dormant in the mind of your buyer. Why reduce your potential?

Is Your Refrigerator Running . . . Updated Virus Software?

In 2000, LG Electronics introduced the world's first Internet-enabled refrigerator.[4] While many new refrigerator-freezers at the time sported water and ice cube dispensers in the door, the Internet Refrigerator offered a few more features. "Based on 'Internet digital DIOS' technology," a press release announced, "the LG appliance is not merely a refrigerator with a built-in notebook, it unites a 'white goods' technology with an animated video telecommunications technology usually used for multimedia products, for the first time in the world." Other features of what LG called the "space-age" appliance included:

✦ TFT-LCD (thin-film transistor, liquid crystal display) screen with TV functionality and Local Area Network (LAN) port
✦ Electronic pen, data memo, video messaging, and schedule management functions
✦ Information about the refrigerator and its contents, such as inside temperature, the freshness of stored foods, nutrition information, and recipes
✦ A Webcam that doubled as a scanner, to scan food in and out and keep up with exactly what inventory was in the refrigerator and how long it had been there
✦ Programmable interface to automatically send out orders, provided that the nearby grocery shops were online
✦ MP3 player for music storage and playback
✦ Three-level automatic icemaker for ice cubes, crushed ice, or cold water

We asked a simple question: What problem was the Internet Refrigerator supposed to solve? Lack of space in the kitchen area, maybe (because you don't have room for both a fridge and a computer)? Well it seems to us that if you can afford an $8,000 Internet Refrigerator, you can probably afford a bigger kitchen. And we doubt it's a good solution to the space problem anyway. Imagine your kids watching TV on the fridge while you're preparing dinner.

Maybe the unit reduces the time you spend on household chores? Well, do you really want to set up a complete supply chain–management system for the items in your refrigerator, complete with RFID-enabled groceries that allow this Superfridge to detect your grocery needs, log on to safeway.com, and then automatically arrange delivery to your house? Would this save time? Is this really a practical solution to your problems?

No, of course not. The Internet Refrigerator is a classic case of guessing—of tuned out, inside-out behavior. The Internet Refrigerator is also a classic case of innovation for innovation's sake and a great example of a product development failure. When organizations are not tuned in, the products and services they create just don't resonate. But it can be much worse. Often the tuned out company so annoys potential customers that they just go away.

Is It a Resonator?

As you get comfortable with the Tuned In Process, you'll soon begin to spot resonators. And you'll also find many examples of products and services, as well as the related company experiences, that just don't resonate. It becomes a bit of a game to spot tuned out behavior:

 **Make them groan when they open it:** Opening a product shipped with packing "peanuts" is a miserable experience. First you have to dig your hands in and fish around to get all the items out of the box. Then you spend days picking up strays because the damn things fly all over the place. (Plus, they are terrible for the environment.) Companies that ship with packing peanuts do so for their own convenience; they're tuned out to their customers.

 **Lock up your label:** Artists whose music was distributed on CDs by Sony BMG Music Entertainment in 2005 faced boycotts of their label when it was learned that digital rights management software was installed from CDs onto users' computers. The software even contained code that had the potential to cripple computers.[5] Message boards lit up with fans' frustrations. Attorneys general in many states, including New York and Texas, sued

Sony BMG in class actions on behalf of consumers. Sony, while perfectly within its rights to protect ownership rights to the music it distributed, went too far and alienated consumers because the company was not tuned in to the buyers of their music and what was important to them.

Make them walk a mile to get to you: When customers arrive at shopping malls in the morning, they often find the lots already filled with hundreds of cars crowded around the entrances. "Why?" the customers wonder. "The stores aren't even open yet." It turns out that many shopping malls allow employees of their stores and restaurants to park in the choice spots. How easy would it be for mall operators to create a policy that encourages store employees to tune in to their potential customers' problem of finding a decent place to park?

Force them to do it your way: For at least the past five years (basically as long as we can remember), when we go to our ATM machine we always get $200 in cash. This is the procedure we endure: first swipe the bank card, enter a PIN number, and select "Get Cash" (because the amount of money we require is not in the "Fast Cash" selection). Then we are confronted with the same options each time—we can select $20, $40, $60, $80, or $100. Since our desired amount is not there, we press "Another Amount" and then manually enter our request for $200. Why can't the ATM machine remember that each time we want cash, we ask for $200? How difficult would it be to offer that as a selection? Is the company that made the ATM machine tuned out to the buyer persona that withdraws more than $100 at a time? Or is it the bank? Or both?

Make them work to find you: Many organizations insist on using antiquated letters for their phone numbers, years after some phone manufacturers stopped putting letters on keypads. Worse, they often fail to include numerals next to the letters when written, so it takes people quite a long time to work out what the phone number for, say, 1–555-TUNED-OUT actually is. While we're all for memory devices that make it easy for people to recall a phone number, the problem with this approach is the frustration many people have with translating the letters to numbers. Another frustration is that some companies use unusual spellings of company names and other words in the "phone number," making it difficult to figure out what number to call. (Some companies even exploit this confusion. Over $300,000 worth of the calls intended for AT&T's 1–800-OPERATOR number actually went to rival MCI's 1–800-OPERATER).[6] These practices make it less likely that many people will actually place the call.

 **Scare them away from your events:** The Washington, DC Metrorail stops running at midnight on weekdays, even on evenings when there is a late football game, concert, or other event in town. Thus, fans cannot use public transportation and so bring more cars downtown, leading to parking problems. For a city, like most, that is looking for ways to keep people in town after work (to support the local business community), is there ever a reason to stop a critical service like public transportation?

We laugh about some of these examples, but then we ask a serious question: how do business leaders let these things happen? The common failing here is cultural. All of these examples illustrate practices that make things easier for the company rather than the customer. We can only conclude that either these companies don't care or they got caught guessing.

Stop Guessing

The best predictor of business success is a focus on the Tuned In Process—an outside-in, market-driven approach. But we recognize that it isn't always easy to be tuned in. There's that gravitational force that wants to suck you back to being tuned out. Thus, we've devised a simple exercise to help you remind yourself to stay tuned in.

Your business must be continuously problem solving for your market.

Question: what business are you in? You'd probably answer by saying you're in the accounting business, or the shoe business, or the enterprise software business. *And you'd be wrong.* If you are a tuned in organization, you should answer, "We're in the business of continuous problem solving for our market." It's remarkable how that simple thought—the way you describe your business—helps to transform your mind and keep you tuned in.

Once we accept that definition for our business, it becomes evident that to survive we must understand the problems our prospective clients' experience. These problems are what should drive companies. In the next chapter, we'll introduce the Tuned In Process. Subsequent chapters will then go into much greater detail on each step of the process, providing examples of tuned in organizations that are creating their own success.

Chapter Summary

✦ Of all the causes of tuned out behavior, the most common we've observed is the logical (but incorrect) assumption that, because you're an expert in a market or industry, you therefore know more than your buyers about how your product can solve their problems.

✦ Most companies have a single dominant focus that drives their approach to business, a "company personality" that determines how each structures itself and behaves in the market.

✦ The most successful organizations are tuned in, operating from a market-driven approach.

✦ Debunking the myth of the innovation-driven organization: when these companies chase innovation for its own sake, they neither satisfy customers nor drive unit sales growth.

✦ Debunking the myth of the sales-driven organization: these companies can juice sales for a while, but the added investment in more and more sales resources means that profitability and customer satisfaction often suffer.

✦ Debunking the myth of the customer-driven organization: these companies limit their market to just the people who already do business with them, and so end up failing to grow.

✦ A focus on any of these approaches—being a customer-, revenue-, or innovation-driven company—*is more risky*. It is possible to build success, but the odds are stacked against you.

✦ Our research shows that *tuned in organizations are in the distinct minority.*

✦ There is a "gravitational force" that tends to pull companies back to being tuned out, as if that were their normal state. Staying tuned in is difficult, much like staying on an exercise program. This is not a natural way for people to think and behave (at least at first).

✦ We've got a simple saying that we use again and again when meetings and discussions fall victim to the inevitable gravitational force that draws groups away from the Tuned In Process: *Your opinion, although interesting, is irrelevant.*

+ The old tuned out way of operating is just easier. But organizations that develop products without first understanding market problems and buyer personas introduce a significant element of risk to their businesses.
+ Your business must be a continuous problem solver for your market.

CHAPTER

3

 # Get Tuned In

How do we build, market, and sell
what our market will buy?

I n 1999 nobody realized that a serious market problem had created the opportunity for a rental car company to develop a
breakthrough product experience. After all, the last big innovation
in the rental car business came in 1946—the year when Warren E.
Avis, a Michigan car dealership owner who was tired of waiting for
taxis outside airports, opened Avis Airlines Rent-A-Car System in
Florida and Michigan.[1] At the time, rental car companies were located in downtown garages. But as a *tuned in* executive, Avis understood the problems facing business travelers, and he pioneered the
practice of offering rental cars at airports. His new service resonated
with thousands of customers in the first few years and became a billion dollar company as a result. Fifty years later, it appeared to many
that Avis had discovered the last extraordinary opportunity in the
rental car marketplace.

And then along came Robin Chase and Antje Danielson. Intrigued by a membership-based car-sharing concept they encountered while on vacation in Berlin, Chase and Danielson returned
home to the Boston area and interviewed city residents about their
driving habits. They asked these residents about car ownership and

their use of rental cars. And they *tuned* in to the urban lifestyle and how it dictated car use—daily, during weekends, and on holidays. The market problem identified by Chase and Danielson? Urban drivers who did not want the hassles of owning a car didn't find it convenient to use existing rental car companies. But they still needed a set of wheels for an hour or two every now and then.

Armed with a wealth of new knowledge, Chase and Danielson launched Zipcar in 2000.[2] They built their new rental car company around an innovative membership system that resonated with the market. Zipcar members log on to their accounts online to reserve cars and authorize use automatically using wireless technology. Members pay a monthly fee, plus a usage charge each time they use a car for a run to Home Depot or Costco, a visit to Aunt Millie in the suburbs, or even a trip to the airport to pick up a friend.

Listening to Your Existing Customers Is Not Enough

We find it fascinating—though hardly surprising—that new market entrants so often create the breakthrough experiences and develop a resonator. Why didn't one of the existing rental car companies in the 1940s create branches at airports? In the late 1990s, why didn't Hertz or National or Enterprise or Budget or any of the other rental car companies grasp that there was a large group of urban buyers ready to pay for a car that they could rent by the hour? Come to think of it, why didn't marketers at Avis, who brought us the original rental revolution, maintain their innovative tradition in the 1990s by launching a product for urban drivers? For so many markets, why does it so often require new companies to solve existing market problems?

While we don't have any direct knowledge of what was happening inside rental car company headquarters in the late 1990s, we do know most organizations tend to tune out after their first success. They don't get out into the marketplace and talk with people to discover and understand new problems that need solving. Instead, they make product and market decisions based on experience or gut feelings, on research reports written by third-party analysts, on articles in industry trade journals, and on customer requests and feedback forms. Companies of all kinds just aren't organized in a way that helps them understand the problems that people are prepared to pay money to have solved for them.

So what was going on at the big rental car companies at the time? Taking a look at the services they now offer, we suspect they did exactly what the vast majority of companies do: focus on incremental improvements to their existing services for their existing customers. This is typical. Instead of discovering the market that Zipcar pioneered, the existing rental car companies focused on strategies like opening offices in new cities and new countries, introducing new lines of luxury or sporty rental cars, installing navigation systems, and adding other incremental service improvements designed to please the current market. While these improvements are nice for existing customers, they are not breakthrough experiences that resonate, and they don't build new markets. This lack of true innovation means that, in order to grow, the rental car companies all spend millions and millions of dollars on expensive advertising to try to build business. Since all the big rental car companies spend big bucks on advertising, it all essentially cancels out, bringing no one success.

When Chase and Danielson developed Zipcar, they studied the requirements of urban drivers: an untapped market segment. They didn't try to outdo the existing companies in their own markets. They interviewed urban drivers rather than relying exclusively on intuition, competitive intelligence, research from the experts, or the advice of smart friends. And because they had no existing market with current customers to focus on (or be distracted by), they directly observed the problems of *potential* customers who were not being served by the existing companies in the rental car space.

We're convinced that if any of the existing rental car companies had been tuned in to this new market and the unresolved problems its buyers had, then any one of them could have created a Zipcar-like offering. But they didn't.

It's Not a Rental Car, It's a Zipcar

Once the Zipcar founders understood their market's problems, they created a breakthrough product experience to solve them. When they need to use a car, Zipcar members view car availability and make a reservation via the Web.

Each vehicle has a home location (a dedicated parking space located on a city street, driveway, or neighborhood lot) in the member's area. Members are issued a "Zipcard" access card, which, when swiped, opens the vehicle (but only at the appointed reservation time) and records the hours of usage, the mileage, and the time of return. This data is then uploaded to a central computer via a wireless data link, charging the member's account. The Zipcar experience resonates so well that many members write about Zipcar on their blogs and have posted YouTube fan videos detailing their experiences.[2]

But the company didn't stop there. In subsequent years, Zipcar developed an understanding of other buyers who would benefit, and the company now offers its services to college students. They've partnered with over thirty colleges and universities, including the 25,000-student University of North Carolina at Chapel Hill, to provide students with access to the Zipcar car-sharing service on or near campus. And they have started a "Z2B" program—Zipcar for Business—that companies can offer to employees as a benefit and that landlords can offer to tenants.

Members aren't the only ones who love the way Zipcar fits their lifestyles—municipalities do too. Several cities offer free parking spots for Zipcars, which provide a green alternative to individual vehicle ownership. With initial service in Boston quickly expanding to 14 cities (including New York, Washington, DC, Minneapolis, San Francisco, Toronto, London, Chicago, and Vancouver), Zipcar has grown into the largest car-sharing organization in North America and Europe. At a time when the U.S. rental car business was flat, Zipcar grew from 5,000 members and $2 million revenue in 2003 to 180,000 members and $100 million in revenue by the end of 2007.

How Zipcar Tuned In and Created a Resonator

The six-step Tuned In Process that we've developed is simple to learn. We're certain that if you apply these six steps to your own business, you will have a much better chance at success. But applying the process means adopting a new approach to how you develop and build products and how you market and sell them. Compared

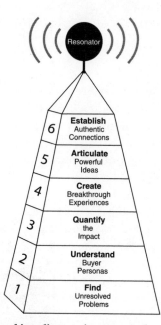

The process of getting tuned in relies on six steps, each providing a foundation for the next and building toward launching a resonator, the perfect solution to a market problem.

with the other ways that companies can organize, following the six tuned in principles (and discussed in detail in the following chapters) is one of the biggest predictors of success. Ignoring them is much more likely to lead to failure.

Zipcar is a wonderful example of a tuned in organization, so we will use this resonator to illustrate the Tuned In Process. The leaders of Zipcar identified an unresolved problem in the marketplace, a problem that people were willing to spend money to solve. They built a successful product experience around this problem, and they communicated to prospective customers using language that resonated with them. Here, then, are the six principles. Throughout the rest of the book, we've provided a more detailed chapter on each principle, together with many examples of successful tuned in companies.

Step 1—Find Unresolved Problems

How do we know what market and product to focus on?

 The critical first step to becoming tuned in is to understand, in great detail, what existing market problems your organization could solve. The only way to accomplish this is to get out of your office. Leading companies interview potential customers and study how they live and work. They understand exactly what people need by digging deep into their lives. When Chase and Danielson first started working on the idea for a new entry into the rental car business, they studied how people actually live and work in cities, and how city dwellers use transportation. They interviewed potential customers about their use of rental cars and about what was frustrating about the experience. Chase and Danielson directly observed the problems of potential customers in the marketplace.

"We knew that we had hit on an idea that was exactly right in terms of demand," says Robin Chase, cofounder of Zipcar. "And it was exactly what the Internet was made for and what wireless technology was made for. I did a lot of online research about other rental car companies, and I also did a lot research into car ownership in Boston to understand who owned cars and who didn't. When I spoke about the concept with urban people who did not own a car, everyone said, 'Oh my gosh, how obvious!'" Chase knew she had an idea that resonated, that she was building Zipcar to solve a real problem in the market. "People were behind me in that first year because so many people liked the idea," she says.

Tuned In leaders understand the complete picture of market problems *before* developing any products. They create solutions in the context of unsolved problems that people would be willing to pay money to solve. Product managers, executives, and marketers regularly meet with people in the marketplace and observe how those people do business or go about their lives. These observations provide insight into the full scope of the problem and the usage requirements and significant obstacles to adoption of any proposed solution. The most important thing they do is to live in and observe the prospect's world.

Step 2—Understand Buyer Personas

How do we identify who will buy our offering?

A buyer persona represents a definable group of people who share one or more problems. Tuned in companies use buyer personas as a core of their product development, marketing, and communications efforts. Product experiences and personalized communications created especially for buyers are much more likely to bring success than one-size-fits-all, generic products and services that appeal to nobody. Developing a profile for each buyer persona is how successful companies catalog what members of this group have in common, how they think, and what really matters to them. Creating a well-defined set of buyer personas and creating a profile for each one eliminates the agony of guessing how to communicate with buyers.

For example, today Zipcar appeals to a number of buyer personas:

+ City dwellers who occasionally need to use a car for a few hours
+ Mayors, city councilors, and police who deal with parking constraints in major cities
+ University administrators who wish to set up a car share service for students
+ University students who occasionally need a car for a few hours
+ Landlords who might offer a car share service as a benefit for tenants
+ Business managers who might want to set up a car share service as a perk for employees

Once you start tuning into your buyer personas, it becomes obvious that the market problems for each are very different. Someone who lives in a city and doesn't own a car but occasionally needs one has very different priorities and problems than the owner of a 100-unit apartment complex who has limited parking availability. A buyer persona profile forms a basis for you to understand target buyers. Instead of just pushing your product, you see market problems through your buyers' eyes and can understand and respond to how they make decisions.

Step 3—Quantify the Impact

How do we know if we have a potential winner?

 Now that you've found a compelling problem to solve and know who might buy your solution, your next task is measurement. Don't stop with measuring how many people have this problem. Tackle questions like these: is the problem you've identified urgent? Is it pervasive in the marketplace? Would buyers pay money for you to solve this problem for them?

In the case of the market problems that Zipcar identified, it was fairly easy to get additional basic information about populations in cities like Boston, Vancouver, London, and Chicago from census data. If you were repeating their research, you would also be able to learn how many private automobiles are registered in each city and, with a quick Google search or a look in the yellow pages, you could get information about existing rental car companies.

"We learned that Americans spend 18 percent of their income on cars," says Chase. "And at the time we were developing the initial product, cell phones were used by 25 percent of the population [and] 40 percent had access to the Web." These numbers were especially promising for Chase because the sort of urban, plugged-in consumers that made up Zipcar's initial buyer persona was already part of that 40 percent who were Web enabled. "We could push everyone to the Zipcar Web site for more information," Chase says. "And if they weren't on the Web already, then they just weren't our target market. I was willing to take the risk and develop Zipcar because the trends were going up."

Identifying if the market problem is urgent and pervasive and if people would be willing to pay to solve the problem requires interviews or perhaps selective surveys of the people who make up each buyer persona. All this collected data makes up the raw material for quantifying the impact of a product offering and building a business case. But unlike mere guesswork or personal feelings about what is "cool," the tuned in data is based on market problems you've identified within definable buyer personas, and you now know whether people are willing to pay money to solve those problems. What's more, you also know how many of these potential customers are out there and how you should communicate with them. Now you can use this information to help you make critical decisions. Should our company create an experience to solve this problem, or abandon this idea? How can we convince the management team that this idea is attractive and potentially profitable? Or should I quit my job and start my own company to create this product? If so, how can I recruit investors to help me develop the idea?

When Chase was first presenting her ideas to venture capital firms, she was met with skepticism. "The VCs said it was too high risk," she says. "They told me all the reasons why it wouldn't succeed. They said, 'The first time someone sees a potato chip bag in one of the cars, they won't rent anymore.'" But the VCs were just stating their opinions. Armed with data and her knowledge that the urban non–car-owning population was supportive of her idea, Chase used her data to persuade a group of early investors to fund the start-up.

Step 4—Create Breakthrough Experiences
How do we build a competitive advantage?

Building a true competitive advantage that allows you to succeed even in a crowded, established market (like the rental car business) requires you to create a breakthrough experience by leveraging what we call your company's *distinctive competence:* that special way you solve customer problems that the competition is unable or unwilling to solve. This competence can take many forms and may include unique business models, product attributes, distribution and sales methods, training, customer service, innovation, quality, or other factors.

Zipcar developed a distinctive competence in *rental car technology,* a technology that the existing companies, such as Avis, Hertz, and National, chose to ignore. Zipcar outfitted each car with wireless equipment and had a Web-enabled reservation procedure that allowed them to create a hassle-free reservation and car access system for members.

"Zipcar was one of the very first companies to think about how to really use wireless technology," says Chase. "The online and Web aspects of our business were fundamental and critical aspects of the business model. For the business to work, the hourly rental reservation and payment process had to be trivial for members to transact online, and it had to be virtually zero cost to the company for each transaction. Contrast that to the typical human rental agent at the time, which cost 6 percent to 10 percent of each car rental." The distinctive competence Zipcar developed around technology meant the company had to create lots of new technological processes. "We had to make the connections between the car itself on the streets and the server logs back at the company," she says. "We made the fundamental decision to eliminate a complex user interface from within the car, and stuck with a simple proximity card held to the windshield."

Does your company have great customer service? Or top-notch training? Are you always first to market? Is your technology the most sophisticated? By identifying and leveraging your distinctive competence to develop products for your buyers, you'll develop competitive advantage.

Step 5—Articulate Powerful Ideas

How do we establish the memorable concepts that speak to the problems buyers have?

In step five of the Tuned In Process, you develop the words and phrases you will use to articulate ideas to your buyers, basing them on what you want your buyers to know about your organization, products, and services. These expressions are *not* just a listing of the features and benefits of your product. And they are *not* merely taglines or slogans dreamed up by an agency. When you follow the first four steps of the Tuned In Process, you're armed with a great deal of information about your buyers and the problems they want solved. The next step requires getting to the core of your offering so that your description of it resonates with your buyers. As these real examples of powerful ideas for individual buyer personas (taken directly from the Zipcar Web site) illustrate, the Zipcar experience resonates with buyers:

✦ "Zipcar is as easy as getting cash from an ATM" (resonates with people who understand the hassles of renting a car).

✦ "Zipcar satisfies all my driving needs at a fraction of the cost of owning a car" (resonates with university students).

✦ "With each Zipcar replacing over twenty privately owned vehicles, we're changing the urban landscape" (resonates with city government officials).

✦ "You probably have tenants you never want to lose—tenants who pay the rent on time, live responsibly, appreciate their living space, and value having you as a landlord" (resonates with owners of apartment buildings).

✦ "Imagine the world with a million fewer cars on the road. We do" (resonates with the environmental movement, whose members can tell the Zipcar story and spread the company's ideas).

What makes these ideas about the Zipcar product resonate is that they were specifically tailored to speak to each buyer persona. This type of thinking represents a very different approach (and attitude toward customers!) than that of a typical company where employees sit in conference rooms developing egotistical mission statements. The tuned in approach is not about "messages" that an advertising agency dreams up in a vacuum, and it's not about taglines and company "vision." No, tuned in organizations stand out from the pack simply because they focus on the ideas that resonate with what individual markets value most.

Step 6—Establish Authentic Connections

How do we tell our buyers that we've solved their problems so they buy from us?

 Tuned in organizations communicate directly with their potential customers. They understand buyers and the primary media those buyers rely on, and then they develop information that buyers *want* to consume. Tuned in companies understand when and where buyers look for answers to their problems, both online and off. They know if buyers search Google, read online portals and

news sites, listen to bloggers' advice and opinions, pay attention to word of mouth from peers and friends, or visit company Web sites. They know if customers read magazines and newspapers or if they check out the bulletin board in the college dorm.

The Zipcar Web site, for example, contains information for each one of their buyer personas: city dwellers, university students, landlords, and so on. Each buyer persona gets personalized information designed to resonate with that group. And Zipcar is also tuned in to offline communications. For example, the company knows that its buyers like "cool cars," so the fleet includes MINI Coopers and Volkswagen Beetles. But, unlike traditional rental cars, each has a Zipcar logo and Web address, making the actual car a communication tool that helps curious observers learn more. Many of the cars are painted in the signature Zipcar light green (which also signals the environmentally friendly aspects of the product experience). By partnering with city government, universities, landlords, and business owners, Zipcar has a dedicated team of customers who evangelize the company to potential renters; this approach itself is another communications strategy that resonates with buyers.

"Marketing can consume giant amounts of money, so we relied on word of mouth and public relations," says Chase. "We recognized the cars themselves are billboards, so we put the Zipcar tagline on the rear and the company logo on the passenger doors of the cars. We had to make the brand like a club brand, a bit exclusive. So the first three cars were VW bugs. We purposely choose cars that were not in the rental car fleet of the big car rental companies—no Ford Taurus, for example—because we needed to be hip and cool."

The Zipcar-as-billboard approach brought an unexpected bonus. "Our first PR megahit that helped to launch the company in a big way was when an Associated Press reporter saw the very first Zipcar on the streets of Boston and called us to do a story," Chase says. The national story "Part-Time Wheels: City Dwellers Share Cars Through New Service" by Heidi B. Perlman ran in the summer of 2000, and hit exactly at the time that Zipcar was launching.

For decades, marketing and public relations have focused on only two ways to get noticed: buy your way in with expensive advertising, or beg your way in by convincing the media to write about your products. Thus, the companies they work for either pay big bucks for ads, trade shows, and direct mail, or rely on PR agencies to send a flurry of press releases to magazines, newspapers, radio, and TV. *The tuned in company is different.* Because tuned in companies understand the market problems that their buyers are willing to pay to have solved for them, and because they have developed real and deep connections with those customers through product experiences that resonate, they are able to create communications programs that buyers are receptive to and actually want to consume. And the traditional media rushes to talk about them.

Launching Products and Services That Resonate

 So those are the six steps to becoming tuned in. Again, this is not an academic exercise or some half-baked theory. These are the principles that have brought success to countless organizations. And while it is *possible* to be successful by following a path different from what we outline here, the risks of these alternatives are much greater.

Launching products that resonate is much easier than bringing products to market in the usual ways. Choosing the *right* sales and distribution process, setting up appropriate pricing models, and communicating the value of your product are all key to unleashing a resonator. Zipcar developed an online model for sales of their membership programs. Of course, they could have opened mall kiosks or storefront operations, or partnered with one of the established rental car companies. Instead, company executives decided that a focus on their distinctive competence (technological savvy) meant that a new membership-based business model using online sales and distribution was best. The base membership level is an occasional driving plan for only $50 per year and $9.00 per hour. People who drive more frequently sign up for monthly commitment plans that start at $50 per month. By making a commitment up front, the hourly rate dips to $8.00. Plans are available up to a $250 per month commitment for the "Zip-Addict," who pays $7.65 per hour.

The Tuned In Process allows organizations of all kinds to make choices about distribution, sales, and pricing that help them meet business goals such as revenue growth and profitability. Being tuned in also allows your company to say "no" to opportunities that might seem attractive on the surface but that actually distract you from the idea that truly resonates. By understanding your buyer personas, you don't "guess" and you don't just push product into the easiest distribution chain. Instead—once again—let your buyer personas be your guide.

The next six chapters will go into detail on each of the steps of The Tuned In Process. We show you proven ways to replicate the process that the executives, marketers, and product developers at Zipcar went through to develop their breakthrough car rental experience and that Shaw used to create and unleash his No Hassle Listing service; we'll teach you how to develop a resonator. We have taught this proven process to tens of thousands of people, and we know the tuned in approach leads to success in today's marketplace. Now we're going to show you how it's done.

Chapter Summary

+ The six-step Tuned In Process that we've developed is simple to learn.
+ Based on extensive experience working with many organizations, we're certain that if you apply these six steps to your own business, you will have a much better chance at success.
+ Step 1—**Find Unresolved Problems** to know what market and which product or service to focus on.
+ Step 2—**Understand Buyer Personas** to understand who will buy your offering.
+ Step 3—**Quantify the Impact** to know if you have a potential winner.
+ Step 4—**Create Breakthrough Experiences** to build a competitive advantage.
+ Step 5—**Articulate Powerful Ideas** to establish the memorable concepts that match up with the problems people have.
+ Step 6—**Establish Authentic Connections** to tell your buyers that you've solved their problems so they buy from you.
+ Your organization's distinctive competence should help you make decisions about how to focus on creating your own resonator.

CHAPTER

4

Step 1: Find Unresolved Problems

How do we know what market
and product to focus on?

I magine an electronics superstore with its rows and rows of tele-
visions all displaying the same channel. How do you choose
which one to buy? Well let's see . . . You could choose a brand you
know and trust, perhaps a Sony or Panasonic. Maybe the salesman
has a recommendation for you to consider. Or you could whip out
your trusty *Consumer Reports* and choose the number one–rated
model. How about the cheapest one? Sure, that's an option too.

Now think for a moment about your personal television habits.
Got any problems your existing TV doesn't solve for you?

Think.

As people first learn the Tuned In Process, many think that collecting market problems must be easy and straightforward. After all,
they say, how difficult can it be to find some potential customers
and ask what problems they have with a specific product or service?
But imagine for a moment that poor TV product manager who

collects problems in the market that he has no ability to solve. What if he called you and asked, "What problems do you have with your television set?"

Over fifteen years, we have asked thousands of people just like you what problems they had with their TV. Most simply stare blankly. Some articulate problems such as: "My TV collects dust" or "I don't like the programming" or "I don't like how the sun shines on the screen."

Then we ask, "Ever lose your remote control?"

In the 1990s, Magnavox *tuned in* to their buyers by studying their problems relating to the television experience. Instead of asking their prospective customers what problems they had, they observed the interaction people had with their TV. They asked in-depth questions about how the TV fit into their life and the family dynamic and compared peoples' relationships with the TV to their other daily activities. And they learned many surprising things about America's love affair with the remote control. In particular, marketing and product management people at Magnavox learned that 80 percent of Americans report losing their remote and more than half of the population loses it up to five times a week. Most reported losing it in or under furniture, but many end up finding it in the most unlikely places (like in the *refrigerator*)![1]

Most people don't volunteer that they have a problem with their remote control because they don't see this as a problem that technology can solve. They blame their spouse or the kids, but not the TV manufacturer. Yet they immediately identify with the problem when prompted.

To solve this problem in the market, Magnavox developed, patented, and introduced the Remote Locator. If you lose your remote, just touch the television's power button and the remote will beep for thirty seconds so you can find it. Unlike electronics gadgets dreamed up by engineers who never actually speak with buyers (the Internet Refrigerator from Chapter 2 comes to mind), the Remote Locator was developed to solve a very real need in the market. Magnavox was *tuned in* to you and your needs (assuming you're part of the vast majority of people who regularly lose the remote).

When the company released the Remote Locator, buyers had something to distinguish the Magnavox model from the others. And it isn't some silly and confusing product feature (like Picture in

Picture); instead it is something that solves a real problem for you. Imagine now visiting your local electronics store, greeted by dozens of TVs, all perfectly adjusted, all on the same channel, and all in the same charcoal-black case. It looks like a commodity market. Then you spot the large sticker on the Magnavox TV that asks, "Ever lose your remote control?"

The Remote Locator was not breakthrough technology and didn't cost a lot of money to develop or manufacture, yet Magnavox created a powerful bias toward their product by solving one small, annoying problem that resonated with 80 percent of the market. Sure, you still might buy the number-one model in *Consumer Reports*, or the cheapest one, or the Sony. But you're certainly intrigued by the Magnavox, right?

Weren't They Just Lucky?

We can relate to the Remote Locator because the three of us have all lost our remotes many times (although none of us have left it in the fridge . . . yet). The Remote Locator resonates with us as consumers, and chances are that you relate too.

But when we tell the Magnavox story in our seminars (and at cocktail parties), someone often challenges us by suggesting that the product people at Magnavox were just lucky. Didn't a bunch of engineers sit in a windowless room somewhere and dream up the idea for the Remote Locator?

No. Magnavox was *tuned in* to their market and created a breakthrough product experience that addressed a problem, one that people were willing to spend money to solve. Magnavox was also tuned in to the best ways to articulate this powerful idea and establish a connection with buyers. How are we so sure? Well, to launch the Remote Locator and build some media buzz, Magnavox released a survey of American households conducted by Opinion Research Corporation:

+ Over half (55 percent) of the respondents said they lost the remote control up to five times a week.
+ After they've lost their remotes, 63 percent of Americans said, they spent up to five minutes per day looking for it.

+ The places where Americans most frequently found their remotes included in the couch or under the furniture (38 percent), in the kitchen or bathroom (20 percent), and, yes, in
  the refrigerator (6 percent).
+ Eighteen percent of women surveyed, compared with just 9
  percent of the men, said that if they had to choose, they
  would rather give up sex than their TV remote control for
  one week. (Editorial comment: yikes!)

Magnavox tuned in to a problem that television buyers really
have (as opposed to adding another ten inches to screen surface
area), created a product experience to solve it, told the market
about the powerful idea (partly through the data in the survey), and
then communicated to the market in ways that people wanted to
hear. The Remote Locator was a resonator.

Looking for Problems

The concept of unresolved market problems may be foreign to people familiar with more traditional ways of developing products and
services. Most organizations probably think up ideas in the shower,
the conference room, or the R&D lab. But what if you took a different approach? What if your organization sent someone—we don't
care what the person's job title is—out into the market on a continuous basis. This person would call on customers but, even more importantly, would meet regularly with noncustomers as well. The
intent would not be to sell anything but to just listen and observe.
The first question might simply be "How's business?" or "What are
your biggest challenges?" What if, through open-ended questions
and good conversations, you began to understand what problems
noncustomers have but can't articulate? How do they get along without your product? How can you leverage your distinctive competence to make their lives better?

Stated Needs and Silent Needs

To be really skilled at finding unresolved problems, you need to
consider two kinds of needs within your buyers—expressed and un-
expressed problems. Sometimes we call these "stated needs" and

"silent needs." Very often, if you can uncover silent needs through skilled interviewing, they end up being the golden nugget of information that will result in a creating a resonator.

Russell Shaw, whom we met in Chapter 1, was skilled at finding out from people what their *stated needs* were. You may recall that he drew up a list of those needs, including things like "I would like to avoid realtor's commissions if I can, but I hesitate to try selling my home myself because of the risks involved," and "If my realtor is not meeting my expectations, I don't want to be stuck with a long-term contract." These are the market problems that buyers freely express to anyone who asks.

However, people at Magnavox, through skilled interviewing, managed to uncover the *silent needs* people had around losing their remote. This process is tricky because, interestingly, people frequently can't articulate a problem directly. However, you might be able to observe, listen, and make an inference. This is particularly true when the person you're speaking with assigns biases based on what your organization does. For example, if a rental car company had approached us, we might talk about what's wrong with rental car companies at airports (because we frequently travel and use rental car companies at airports—that's our bias). So it takes a skilled interviewer to draw out the concepts that would lead to Zipcar.

Did the idea of a Remote Locator resonate with you? This silent need does with many people. Such problems take probing to uncover. After all, if the problem of lost remotes was something people were shouting about to anyone who would listen, then another TV manufacturer would have developed it much sooner. Listen, learn, and see if you can identify problems whose solutions can be turned into product offerings. Remember: had another TV manufacturer thought to ask the right questions, they too could have uncovered the market problems the Remote Locator solves, and created a resonator.

But Our Business Doesn't Solve Problems!

Sometimes when we talk about market problems on the speaking circuit or in our seminars, people will jump in and challenge us on the idea of market problems. Some want to insist that their products don't solve problems, so instead they must do a "missionary sell" or "create the need" so that people will want to buy. Have you ever tried "educating the market" in order to launch your product or service? It's really tough, isn't it? That's because offerings developed via an inside-out, tuned out process don't resonate, so the only hope is to muscle your way in with lots of sales resources and a big advertising budget. Even then, such products are unlikely to succeed.

Other people insist that their product or industry doesn't solve a problem. A typical argument might go like this: "If it were about solving a transportation problem, wouldn't everyone just buy the cheapest car?" Well, no, because cars solve lots of problems besides the need for transportation. Volvo has developed distinctive competence in solving *safety* problem for buyers.[2] An expensive, late-model SUV in your driveway solves the problem of showing the neighbors that you're doing very well financially. Or a red sports car might help solve the problem of finding a date for a middle-aged man on a Saturday night . . .

Show Me How You Write a Check

The idea for Quicken first came to Scott Cook when his wife was complaining about balancing her checkbook. Cook, then an assistant product manager at Procter & Gamble, teamed up with Stanford engineering student Tom Proulx to form Intuit, a company focused on solving the various problems associated with managing personal finances.[3] The duo recognized that the PC would soon offer a replacement for paper-and-pencil personal accounting. But, unlike most entrepreneurs, they didn't just rush out to build a product. Before writing a single line of computer code, Cook *tuned in* to his market by interviewing people to find out how they managed their personal finances. He personally contacted upscale consumers who already owned or were likely to purchase PCs, in order to understand, in great detail, the tedious task of managing a household budget. To gain an even deeper understanding of his potential customers, Cook hired his sister-in-law to contact hundreds more people.

Intuit was *not* the first company to identify the market opportunity. In fact, there were forty-six competitors when Quicken launched (Cook and Proulx joked about having forty-seventh mover advantage). But Intuit enjoyed a tremendous market edge over its competitors. Unlike the other guys, they didn't just guess what buyers needed in a personal finance software product. Instead, through the hundreds of interviews, Cook identified deep insights into what their market valued. Intuit understood that their main competitor was not the other software packages in the market. It was a pencil. A pencil was what people were using at the time, and it was extremely easy to use.

In order to beat a pencil, the team set as its goal that a novice PC user should be able to write a check in Quicken within fifteen minutes of opening the package. By starting with the in-depth interview data, Cook created a new software application that was based on a checkbook metaphor. Thus, Quicken "looked" just like the tool people already used for dealing with their finances. It didn't require them to change any ingrained habits. Quicken created a breakthrough experience for more than fifteen million users.

As Intuit began to grow, the company established "Follow Me Home," a program where Intuit employees regularly observed consumers using the company's products at home. The motto "Right for Me," as in "Right for Me" products and services, was bred into the company culture. This fundamental way of running the company is totally consistent with what we've said several times already in these pages: your opinion, although interesting, is irrelevant. The information Intuit gathered from being tuned in to market problems allowed Intuit to unleash a powerful idea: Quicken ends financial hassles.

Intuit connected with buyers and, because the ideas resonated, Quicken quickly became the bestselling product in the market. At the time of this writing, the company was generating $2.6 billion in annual revenue, growing at 10 percent per year, and basking in its status as one of America's most admired companies and best places to work. By constantly monitoring what's going on in the marketplace and understanding the problems that buyers have, Intuit has consistently met or exceeded business projections since its inception. Wall Street has rewarded the company with a best-in-class stock performance.

Meeting with Buyers

When Scott Cook first built Quicken, he actually went into homes and studied the process of how families paid bills and managed their finances. He didn't rely on intuition, or competitive intelligence, or the advice of smart friends. He also didn't assume that his own problems were universal. Instead, Cook directly observed the problems his potential customers actually had.

By far the best way to collect unresolved market problems is to visit buyers face-to-face in a nonselling situation, in a place where talking about your market category makes sense, and by preference on the buyer's home turf. For example, if your company sells business-to-business products or services, you should meet with buyers in their workplace. If you sell outdoor products for the home market, why not have conversations in people's gardens? A sporting goods manufacturer might go to a team practice or interview travelers at a favorite vacation spot. That's why insurance agents are taught to sit at a customer's kitchen table, the spot where significant family decisions are made.

Setting up such interviews is simple. Contact representatives of your target market by phone, e-mail, or in person. You can find people who are part of your buyer persona by using lists of people who have visited your company at a trade show, by purchasing names from industry magazines, or by looking at the inquiries to your Web site. Say that you have nothing to sell but are simply asking for thirty minutes of their time to better understand how they live (or how their business works, or how they exercise, or how they shop for clothes, or how they take care of their children's meals, or whatever makes sense in your case). Tell them you're trying to learn how to build products that will make them more effective or efficient (or a service to help them have more fun). It is important that, when you make your request, the subjects know you're not in sales. Say something like, "I'm not selling. I'm trying to determine what products to offer next year." One person we know uses the following line: "The sales department won't let me sell. I couldn't sell you anything even if you wanted to buy."

Then you need to ask open-ended questions that you don't have the answers to. Most importantly, you need to listen. Take notes as the person is speaking. Even better, do the interview paired up with someone else. That way, one person can interview and one can write.

Tuned In Buyer Interview Checklist

+ Go in with an open mind. Be prepared to learn something remarkable, something you never knew. You may develop a whole new take on your market.
+ Remember, your buyer is the expert. You are there to observe and to listen.
+ When possible, conduct your interviews on the buyer's turf.
+ Ask open-ended questions: "How do you accomplish that?" or "Why is that important?" or "Who needs that information and why?" or "What purpose does that function serve?" (These are just some ideas. The best approach is to have a conversation rather than using a rigid script, although you may need to use several scripted questions at the outset to get the conversation rolling.)
+ Don't talk about your company or its products!

Again, we often hear from skeptics when we describe this approach. People ask us why buyers would give a complete stranger thirty minutes of their time. Well, we've learned that many people do respond to this approach, and there are two primary reasons. First, people like talking about themselves and their problems, so if you make it perfectly clear that you are not selling anything, then many people will want to speak with you. Second, there are also people who are willing to talk because they think they may help a smart organization create a product that helps solve a problem for them. They think, "Hey, if it makes my life better, I'll give you thirty minutes."

Look for Problems in Your Entire Market, Not Just Your Customer Base

We hear again and again that the secret to success in business is to focus on customers. While we certainly agree that customer service is a good thing and that keeping your existing customers happy can result in more sales, we want to emphasize once again what we said in Chapter 2—that your existing customers are only one component of applying the Tuned In Process.

The best way to create a resonator is to focus on the entire market by categorizing your **buyers** into three segments: your **customers, evaluators,** and **potential customers**. (Throughout the book, we use "buyers" to mean your total market, the entire universe of people you might do business with.)

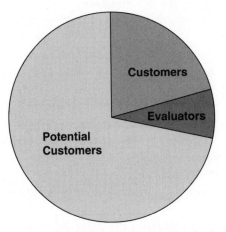

Finding unresolved buyer problems requires a research mix that balances input from existing customers, evaluators, and potential customers—in direct proportion to the size of opportunity.

The exact proportions may vary, but most businesses operate in an environment where customers and evaluators make up a small percentage of the total market. That means you'll need to spend most of your time with potential customers to find your next resonator. Understanding the needs of these three classes of people will give you a broader perspective on the market potential of your future offerings.

Customers

Your existing **customers** have already purchased and implemented your product or service. You know that your organization is already solving one set of problems for them. They know you. As a result, you find problems in the rearview mirror. In other words, you learn how to make incremental improvements to your *existing* products and services. The process of tweaking features to please your existing customers distracts you from getting out to discover unresolved problems in a new or related marketplace.

Many organizations excel at customer support and customer communications, and certainly you will get important buyer input from this channel. Use it! But realize that existing customers will respond to requests with tactical problems or ideas for products that are similar to those that you already deliver.

Your existing customers will be a small but important part of the Tuned In Process. Discussions with them should be channeled to move beyond small incremental improvements and instead focus on the problems that will make your solution complete, and on new problem areas that you can address.

Evaluators

The second category of buyers, your **evaluators**, comprises people who are actively reviewing products and services like the one you sell and are in some way already in your sales cycle. For example, if you sell boats, your evaluators may have visited your company at boat shows, downloaded materials from your Web site, or taken one of your boats for a test spin. If your company has a direct-sales force or distributors with salespeople, then anyone your salespeople are directly communicating with are also evaluators.

Evaluators are a tricky audience to tap into because there is an active sales cycle ongoing. Imagine that you are considering the purchase of a new car in the next week. As you visit dealerships, you have a very particular sort of car in mind. And because you may purchase, you probably won't be completely honest with the dealer. At the same time, the dealer won't want to ask you questions to focus on new product development because those new cars won't be available for a year or more. We recommend that you observe people when they are in the sales process, but don't probe too deeply and don't weigh a request too highly when one does come in. "I'll buy today if the car is lime green" may just be a way to get out the door, not a real request. However, an in-depth interview—what we call win-loss analysis—about a month after someone makes a purchase decision (either to buy your product or to go with the competitor) is often very useful. An independent interview on how purchase decisions are really made and what problems were left unresolved is nearly always candid and eye opening.

Your evaluators are also a small but important audience for your tuned in research. In most organizations, it is best to leave evaluators alone during selling cycles in favor of an in-depth interview later.

Potential Customers

We use the term **potential customer** to describe people who are not yet your customers but who have market problems that your products and services can (or could) solve. For most organizations, potential customers represent by far the largest number of people. Potential customers are your future customers and they represent new revenue for next year and the years after that. In our examples in this chapter—Magnavox and Intuit—company representatives met with potential customers to learn about the market problems that led to the Remote Locator and Quicken.

Your potential customers are the most important category of people to spend time with. What are their problems? What can your company do to solve those problems? Learning about unresolved market problems is the best way to create breakthrough experiences that resonate.

Why Not Have Salespeople Tell Us?

We often hear people say, "We have our own sales force [direct sales, telesales, or via a distribution channel]. Our representatives are talking to prospects all the time. Why can't we just ask the salespeople about the problems in our market?" The flaw in this approach is that the sales situation and salespeople's very skills, are notably poor at finding unresolved problems:

+ Unless your salespeople are picking up the phone and making cold calls, they aren't speaking with the most important group. Instead, they are just communicating with your existing customers and evaluators (those who are already in the sales process).

✦ Salespeople are really great at interviewing one prospect at a time and building empathy with that one person. But this skill makes it difficult for them to translate what they hear from that one person into information for the market as a whole. If one person says he wants red grass, a salesperson will suggest that the company develop a strain of red grass because that will enable them to sell "more of what the customer wants."

✦ Salespeople are great at overcoming objections. This skill means that they are prone to translate market problems into objections that they can shoot down on the spot: "Our green grass can be dyed red." They have difficulty handling any scenario where a client expresses a genuinely unsolved problem without looking at it as an opportunity to convince them to look at the situation differently. Unfortunately, those are the very scenarios the Tuned In Process helps you seek.

Most salespeople must balance the tasks of facilitating the buying process and simply peddling things buyers don't want. In some industries, they struggle mightily with this. (Who really likes walking into an auto showroom?) For this reason, many evaluators hate the selling process and will do almost anything to avoid it. Thus, sending a salesperson to learn about buyer problems can turn a relationship adversarial before the conversation even begins.

You (and Your Family) Are Not Your Buyer

As we emphasized in Chapter 2—*your opinion, although interesting, is irrelevant*. The same goes for the opinions of your family members. We often hear of organizations that use family members as a proxy for interviewing people in the marketplace. A team member might say, "I have a teenager, so I know how teenagers think." No, you don't. Of course, the teenager who lives in your house is definitely a representative of some buyer personas, and you should interview her as part of your research. But she is just one data point in the sample.

Howard Upton, executive vice president of the Petroleum Equipment Institute from 1951 through 1987, tells a story about sitting in a business luncheon with oil industry executives forty years ago.[4] The group was listening to an advertising executive discussing the idea of introducing self-service gas pumps. The executives dismissed the concept because, although they might have been inclined to pump their own gas to save five cents per gallon, they said that their wives would never participate in such an activity. These well-paid executives missed one of the most revolutionary marketing developments in the energy business on the grounds that it wouldn't appeal to their own spouses.

We're convinced that typical organizational culture leads to the same kind of *tuned out thinking*. Nobody interviews people first to learn about market problems. Thus, development efforts result in products that become bloated, overgrown inspirations that company insiders consider cool but that people aren't prepared to plunk down money to buy. However, once a company's leadership focuses on being *tuned in* (paying attention to the needs of the marketplace), they can begin to develop breakthrough products like the iPod—a product that solved an unmet market problem (a lack of easy-to-use MP3 players) and that over a hundred million people were prepared to spend money on.

Other Ways to Find Unresolved Problems

The best way to find unresolved problems is to interview buyers in an appropriate setting. During the interview, you should ask open-ended questions about their lives or work habits to discover problems your organization might solve.

But there are several other ways to conduct research:

✦ In some markets, people meet at conferences and conventions. If your industry holds these events, you might go as a participant (not as a representative of your company if you also have a sales presence at the event). Listen to the proceedings and interact with other participants. During the breaks and meals, start conversations using open-ended starters like "So what brings you to the conference?" Often, you can learn a great deal about what's on people's minds.

✦ With seventy million blogs in the English language, there are bound to be some written by members of your buyer personas.[5] These are people who are passionate about a subject and are eager to share their passion with the world. Read blogs to see if bloggers are discussing unresolved market problems. Often this can yield very important data and is even in a format that you can pull direct quotes for use in your planning meetings and attribute them to each blogger. Use a blog search engine like Technorati, Icerocket, or Google Blog Search to find the blogs that are important for your market.

✦ Speak at conferences and industry events. If you did a good job (and did not try to sell your product from the podium), people will be eager to meet you and talk afterward.

While conferences, events, publications, and blogs are all good ways to learn about unresolved problems, don't let these methods be a substitute for doing direct interviews. The tuned in leader gets out into the marketplace and meets with buyers.

Creating Disneyland

Disneyland wasn't created by an innovator. It came about because Walt Disney himself was tuned in to market problems. Walt visited amusement parks and observed what people were doing. He identified market problems and created Disneyland to solve them.[6]

For instance, existing parks sold individual tickets to each attraction. This practice caused delays, so Disneyland sold books of tickets. Rides were divided into letter categories, running A through E, and so were the tickets: an E ticket got you into an E ride, and so on. Existing parks also had some attractions for adults (the beer tent, for example) and some for kids (rides with small seats). Walt noticed that this tended to break families up, so he banned alcohol and created attractions that the entire family could enjoy together.

Since the existing parks were only open during the summer season, they attracted seasonal "carny" workers. Walt noticed they tended to be transient (and thus did not become skilled at their jobs), as well as gruff, foul-mouthed, and scary to children. Disneyland was the first park to stay open year-round and hire full-time workers, so it could hire the best people. Finally, to further distance Disneyland from existing parks, Walt insisted that "cast members" (not employees) always wear "costumes" (not uniforms) when "on stage" with "guests" (not customers). These semantic differences helped to distance Disneyland from other parks and reinforce the idea that the new Disney park was special.

Walt Disney created a resonator. The Disney theme park experience solved the need for a family-friendly place for some fun and adventure. By getting tuned in to the market, he understood that people wanted a clean, safe park that was more than just a park. "Disney doesn't build rides," he once said. "Disneyland adventures tell stories and sometimes put you on cars, boats, trains, or other vehicles, not for riding but to carry you into and through an exciting story." Disneyland has been a huge hit with families ever since, spawning similar Disney parks in Florida, Tokyo, Hong Kong, and France.

Chapter Summary

+ While it is possible to "luck into" success, the best way is to be *tuned in* to your market, creating a breakthrough product experience that addresses an *unresolved market problem*, one that people are willing to spend money to solve.

+ The concept of unresolved market problems may be foreign to many people who are familiar with more traditional ways of developing products and services, such as thinking up ideas in the shower, a conference room, or the R&D lab.

+ The best way to identify unresolved market problems is to visit buyers face-to-face in a nonselling situation.

+ Your opinion, although interesting, is irrelevant, and so are the opinions of your family members.

+ Nothing important happens in the office; the answer you're looking for is outside your building.

+ There is a fundamental flaw with relying exclusively on your existing customers for input: namely, your existing customers have different market problems than noncustomers (buyers who don't yet do business with you).

+ We refer to **buyers** as the entire universe of people that you might do business with. Buyers include three major subgroups: customers, evaluators, and potential customers.

+ Your organization is already solving problems for your **customers**, so by all means, we encourage great customer support and terrific customer communications. However, don't rely exclusively on customers to help you identify unresolved problems.

+ People who are actively reviewing products and services like the ones you sell and are in some way already in your sales cycle are your **evaluators**, and you should leave them alone and not interview them as part of the Tuned In Process (you don't want to jeopardize a possible sale).

+ People who are not yet your customers—but who have market problems that your products and services can (or could)

(*continued*)

solve—are your **potential customers**, and they are the most important category of people to spend time with.

+ Don't use your salespeople for conducting buyer interviews because they are not skilled at this kind of interviewing.

+ As a secondary source of information about unresolved problems, you can meet people at conferences and other events and read the publications and blogs that they read. But don't let these methods become a substitute for doing face-to-face interviews.

CHAPTER

5

Step 2: Understand Buyer Personas

How do we identify who will buy our offering?

The Nalge Company was founded to produce high-quality laboratory equipment. One of the company's bestsellers has been the durable, shatter-resistant, lightweight Nalgene-brand plastic water bottle. Available in many different shapes and sizes, the bottles were originally designed and sold for lab use, catching on because they are lighter than glass and protect against leakage, breakage, and contamination. For many years, the bottles were only available in translucent white.

But then something remarkable happened.

Nalgene bottles began venturing into the great outdoors, as scientists and lab workers liberated them from the laboratories and for use on camping trips and wilderness expeditions. Soon the bottles began appearing at Boy Scout campouts and similar events. And everyone wanted to know where the rugged, lightweight, and incredibly useful containers came from. As a result, the president of the company tuned in to the unresolved problems of a completely new buyer persona and decided right then to begin offering Nalgene bottles to explorers, adventurers, and campers around the globe. The *exact same product* that had been sold to one buyer persona (scientists and laboratory workers) transformed into a product for another, entirely different buyer persona by being marketed and distributed through outdoor retailers such as EMS and REI.

Soon Nalgene bottles started appearing on college campuses. The bottles solved a problem by allowing students to carry water from class to class in their backpacks and to have water nearby when holed up in the library. Other students noticed, and minifads started to pop up at some schools. The company tuned in to yet another buyer persona—this time understanding that college students craved some personalization and variety—introducing a new line of colored Nalgene bottles specifically aimed at the campus market. Significantly, the colored bottles were offered at nearly twice the price of the translucent white ones. The company also implemented a private label program where colleges and universities could put their college shield on the bottle (but always with the Nalgene logo too). The private-label program ensured that the bottles were stocked in college bookstores right on campus.

You might guess what happened next. As the green environmental movement caught on, the company tuned in to anther important buyer persona for Nalgene bottles. Many environmentally conscious people see purchased bottled water as harmful to the environment because of the fuel required to transport the water and the billions of empty water containers being dumped at landfill sites. Recognizing the market problems of this new buyer persona, the company launched a new initiative for the green market in 2007. Called "Refill Not Landfill," the campaign encourages people to refill their Nalgene bottles instead of purchasing bottled water. The company also released specially designed versions of the Nalgene bottles with the new Refill Not Landfill logo.

Same Product, Different Buyer Personas

In each case, *the Nalgene product is essentially the same,* but the market problems it solves for each buyer personas are very, very different.[1] For the buyer persona in the lab market, Nalgene bottles solve workplace problems. The lab bottles are commonly purchased in bulk quantities through a central purchasing department, and the company has a Web site at nalgenelabware .com for this buyer persona. For the adventurer, the bottles solve problems associated with people's passion for the outdoors; if carrying water is less of a hassle, the overall camping experience improves. Campers purchase the bottles at retail, perhaps a couple at a time. Nalgene has a site especially for this buyer persona too, at nalgene-outdoor.com.

College students have yet another set of market problems: staying hydrated during long days of classes and studying. The option of purchasing bottled water is expensive, so Nalgene bottles have exploded in popularity on campus. They are easy to buy, typically cost around $8 each, and are available (in many colors) right at the university bookstore—and hey, the student's college bookstore account is paid by Mom and Dad. Finally, the Refill Not Landfill initiative specifically targets the buyer persona in the green movement with a special site at refillnotlandfill.org. The Refill Not Landfill educational initiative provides information to consumers ("on average, one person uses 166 disposable plastic water bottles each year") and encourages people to make small changes toward a big difference in reducing the amount of waste-disposable water bottles contribute to landfills each year.

The professionals in charge of the Nalgene brand are clearly tuned in to their buyer personas. They've articulated powerful ideas and made connections with buyers about a product that *resonates in different ways with different buyer personas*. The Nalgene color bottles have sold very well, with significantly more than one million color bottles sold in the first few years to the new buyer personas the company developed. The bottle has established a cultlike following, with many people posting on blogs and forums about their love of the product. Quite a few videos highlighting the indestructible nature of the bottle have appeared on YouTube—people try to destroy the bottles in wacky ways like running over them with trucks and dropping them from tall buildings. Countless consumers have a real feeling of ownership for the Nalgene brand, and the passion people feel for this resonator means that company employees have to safeguard the brand. In the face of cheap knockoffs from Asia, the company maintains exclusivity by limiting the sales distribution to specialty stores, campus bookstores, and the company's Web sites, but they exclude big retailers like Wal-Mart.

By getting tuned in to different buyer personas, marketers at the company transformed their product from a piece of well-respected laboratory equipment into the container-of-choice for wilderness adventurers, campers, college students, and the environmentally conscious. The key to creating a resonator and selling millions of bottles was developing buyer personas beyond the initial lab market, focusing on the problems that a quality bottle could solve, developing product experiences that resonated, and establishing connections to each buyer persona.

The Importance of Buyer Personas

Tuned in organizations understand that the best way to develop products and services that resonate is to identify the unresolved problems of a particular group of people. By breaking buyers into distinct groups, understanding what problems those groups (or "buyer personas") have and how to solve them, and then cataloging everything you know about each buyer persona, your hard work becomes easier. You are more likely to create breakthrough experiences, articulate powerful ideas about what your organization can do, and establish connections with people. This approach is utterly different from what most organizations do: either not segmenting the market at all (creating nonspecific offerings and marketing them to everyone) or segmenting based on their own egotistical view of the world.

Think about the hotel industry. Most people who run hotels think their business is selling hotel rooms for customers to sleep in at night, and also providing meeting rooms and places to eat. The tuned out approach these hotels use to create products and deliver information to potential customers results in boring offerings and advertising based on the hotel's particular idea of what's important— stuff like fluffy pillows and tasty shrimp. But if you think about the various buyer personas who purchase hotel services, you immediately recognize a different way to create experiences and market them to the people whose problems hotels solve. For example, consider the following hotel buyer personas and note how different their problems are:

✦ Independent business travelers make their own decisions about which hotel to stay in when they visit a city. Perhaps this buyer persona requires a clean and safe room in the city center with a wireless Internet connection and a parking garage.

✦ In-house travel departments, found at many companies, cut deals with hotel chains and then book their travelers in these preferred hotels. When company travel departments are the buyer persona, the problems that a hotel solves are completely different—even though the product (a hotel room) is the same. The travel department focuses on things like reducing overall costs, minimizing paperwork, centralizing the billing, getting free upgrades for executives, and so on.

✦ Organizations of all kinds book hotel meeting rooms for conferences, conventions, seminars, and the like. If the event draws people from out of town, the conference organizers often reserve a block of sleeping rooms too. This buyer persona wants to ensure that the event goes off without a hitch—that the meals are served on time, the AV equipment is in place, the support staff are prepared to assist, and the event comes in under budget. Pragmatic Marketing schedules over one hundred seminars per year at hotels in or near major cities, and meeting planners take into consideration the meeting room itself. Does it have windows? And, if so, are there curtains or blinds that can be drawn to darken the room for a PowerPoint presentation? Are there columns in the meeting room that, when a classroom-style set is applied, might lead to obscured views for some of the attendees?

✦ Vacation travelers want to enjoy a safe, fun, and hassle-free experience. They're more likely to use the pool, and the more kid friendly these facilities, the better. For this buyer persona, things like a self-service laundry room, swimming pool with a slide, and "kid clubs" where parents can leave the little ones for a few hours are important.

✦ Musicians check into a hotel after the gig at three or four in the morning and need to sleep until afternoon.

✦ Couples planning a wedding reception in the hotel have utterly different problems to solve than the other buyer personas. They want to make decisions on all aspects of the big event, to pick every course of the meal, the color of the tablecloths, the kind of flowers, the great band or DJ that will entertain. (This is very different from many corporate meeting planners' list of important considerations.)

By truly understanding the problems and the mindset of various hotel buyer personas, smart hotels owners and managers can create buyer experiences that are far more powerful and resonant than hotels that just offer a room and a meal. And once the product is created, instead of a one-size-fits-all approach, communications, marketing, Web sites, and perhaps even individual staff members should be allotted to each buyer persona, to reflect the way the hotel experience solves the problems of each group.

Picture-Perfect Weddings

 What picture comes to mind when you think of a wedding? Perhaps an idyllic image of a beautiful bride and smiling groom. Or happy families enjoying a great party in a first-class location. Maybe a tropical beach for the honeymoon.

The reality is something less than perfect. Carley Roney and David Liu tuned in to the *real* picture and identified problems that affected millions of couples every year. Planning a wedding is, after all, an exercise in *extreme* event management and is high stress under the best of scenarios. In crowded markets, the problem of competing with hundreds of other couples for scarce resources (locations, caterers, florists, musicians, and more) can challenge even a seasoned event planner.

In response, Roney and Liu created The Knot, an online wedding planning site that provides to-be-weds (whom they call "Knotties") with first-class wedding planning service.[2] The site includes tons of ideas about reception locations, bride and bridesmaid dress options, tuxedos for groomsmen, photographers, florists, music, and cakes. It also comes with the Wedding Planning Checklist, Wedding Budgeter, Guest List, Notebook, and even a couples' Web site for family members to view event information and gift preferences. Most importantly, The Knot is full of advice, including Roney's columns and forum comments from the millions of members who want to share their experiences.

"Traditional wedding planning services had a number of inherent weaknesses," says Liu. "First, they only provided access to the national brands for services, which were also coincidentally the most expensive and in highest demand. Scheduling and working within budget constraints were real issues for many couples, and no one was supporting that reality. Secondly, they only serviced one image of a wedding where the bride was the Princess of the Day and everyone fully supported the event. We found that a high percentage of couples had to deal with real-world issues of interracial, multi-denominational, [or] second marriage[s]: lack of support from key family members, budget limits, and many more issues that created stress."

By providing an outlet for advice and interaction, The Knot captured more than double the number of subscribers of traditional providers like *Bride* or *Modern Bride*. "The real breakthrough we offered was easy access to a central source of information that was online," says Liu. "But our understanding of our audiences is what sustains us. We're not about being cool or innovative. We're about solving the problems our members have in ways that will cause them to use us every day and not be afraid to ask for new things for fear that it will be too complicated."

This philosophy kept the founders tuned in as their membership expanded and couples who managed their weddings through The Knot kept coming back; today, the company focuses on the problems of new buyer personas—those who want the same kind of help in the next stages of their married life. The Knot expanded by building community subsystems about "Money and Marriage," "Trouble in Paradise," "Sex in Relationships," and "Babies on Board."

"The Nest grew out of this foundation," Liu says. "As marriages moved through their first couple of years, the predominant issue was dealing with the transition of a first child. It created some of the same dynamics for couples that their wedding did in terms of management, need for information, access to expertise, and recommendation on services down to building babies rooms and buying new furniture."

Thus, because Roney and Liu stayed tuned in, "Knotties" became "Nesties" and the company now boasts two successful and thriving communities to serve buyers in both these stages of life.

The Knot went public in 2000 and had earned $82 million in revenue by the end of 2006. The company is growing at a rate of 41 percent per year with profits of 32 percent, and it was number fifteen on the *Fortune* list of the top 100 small businesses in 2007. A free service to its members, the community has a strength and stickiness ideal for the buyer persona that actually pays money to The Knot—the advertisers and sponsors who want to reach members. "Because of the specific nature of our community, value of the brand, and the interest of our members in purchasing services, advertising is sold at a premium," Liu says.

NASCAR Dads and Security Moms

Building buyer personas is one of the most important things that your organization can do to become tuned in. Consider the U.S. presidential elections of 2004, when George W. Bush was fighting for reelection against John Kerry. Operatives for the two major candidates segmented buyers (voters) into dozens of distinct buyer personas. Some of what are called "microtargets" in the political world became well known as the media began to write about these buyer personas. Some better-known buyer personas during this campaign included "NASCAR Dads" (rural, working-class men, many of whom are NASCAR fans) and "Security Moms" (mothers who were concerned about security and worried about terrorism, and who had been "Soccer Moms" in the 2000 election cycle).[3] The campaigns targeted their TV commercials, speeches, direct mail, and PR programs directly to each buyer persona. This buyer persona focus is much more effective than a one-size-fits-all presidential campaign that targets everyone but appeals to no one.

For each buyer persona profile you create, you will develop a document with as much information as you can gather about this group, just like the presidential campaigns did. What are your buyer personas' problems? Are they willing to pay money to solve these problems? What is the ideal product or service that can help them? How can you reach them? What media do they rely on for answers to problems? Simply put, you want to know, in detail, what's important to each buyer persona. As we learned in Chapter 4, the best way to learn about buyers and develop buyer persona profiles is to interview people. We have no doubt that representatives of the two presidential candidates interviewed representatives of their various buyer personas, including NASCAR Dads and Security Moms and many others they identified.

Grok Your Buyer Personas

So important is the idea of developing buyer personas that we use a word to describe the process: grok (it rhymes with "rock"). Grok originated with the 1961 novel *Stranger in a Strange Land* by Robert A. Heinlein. We use grok as a verb that captures the essence of what we strive to achieve through buyer persona profiles. Once you've grokked a buyer persona, you know as much about these buyers as they know about themselves. The first step is to interview buyers, as we outlined in Chapter 4. Next, put yourself into their world as much as possible, so you can begin to know how they think. Grokking is more than just listening and acting on what you hear. Instead, we challenge you to understand your buyers so deeply that you anticipate those market problems that people can't even articulate (like Magnavox did with the Remote Locator).

We encourage you to name your buyer personas, the way the campaigns labeled NASCAR Dads and Security Moms did. A hotel might name buyer personas something like "Independent Ernie," "Wedding Wendy," and "Corporate Carol." You might even cut out a representative photo from a magazine to help you visualize him or her. One of our clients considers buyer personas so important that framed representative photos and bios of them hang in the employee cafeteria. Clearly, you must keep the buyer persona profile, name, and photo internal to your organization. It is a tool that you use to develop empathy with and a deep understanding of the real people whom you solve problems for. Rather than a nameless, faceless "prospect," your buyer persona will come to life.

We'll admit that it isn't easy to achieve this level of insight. Many organizations attempt to shortcut the process by hiring people into their marketing or product development departments who are former customers. They think that having one representative of the buyer persona on staff is enough. But every individual's prior experiences are limited to a small number of companies, and relying on one "in-house expert" inevitably misrepresents the market as a whole. And even if the ex-customer is knowledgeable about your buyer persona, the key phrase here is "ex-customer." On joining your company, the individual leaves the industry and instantly becomes dated. No buyer persona is ever complete. Grokking a buyer persona isn't a project with a distinct beginning and end. Your goal is to commit to an ongoing process where you continue to learn more and gain deeper insight into your buyer personas.

A Camera for Surfers

 If you search an online marketplace such as Amazon for "waterproof digital camera," you'll see that most models look essentially the same—a normal camera within a waterproof housing of some kind. But suppose you're a surfer who wants to capture the experience on camera. You're on your board in pounding surf that requires your focus to stay in position. When a wave approaches, you've got just a second or two to manage your board, and you need both your hands to paddle. If you get an opportunity to take a photo, you need to quickly position the camera and click off a shot without losing your camera in the process. As any surfer would know, it's almost impossible to haul around a standard camera, especially in big waves.

"Traditional cameras are not designed for surfing, skydiving, or riding a bike, so people could only capture the famed 'parking lot photo' before and after the event," says Nicholas Woodman, founder and CEO of GoPro.[4] "The larger camera companies are building product on such a massive scale that it is not interesting to sell to a small niche market. When you're building a camera for a market potential of ten million units, it doesn't seem worth the time to build a product for a hundred thousand people."

Woodman was frustrated that he couldn't indulge in his passion for video and photography at the same time as his love for surfing. "On a three-month surf road trip to Australia, the product idea for GoPro was kicking around in my head," he says. "Then I returned home, extending my trip up and down the California coast in my mobile office, a 1974 VW Campmobile, and I wrote the initial patent drafts for what became the GoPro Digital HERO 3 camera." Unlike all the other waterproof digital cameras, this unit fastens to a surfer's wrist with a Velcro strap in a manner that allows the camera to be locked between flat and upright positions, depending on if the surfer is paddling or is shooting photos and video. "GoPro's cameras are more specialized and complement your regular camera," Woodman says. "You still take your Canon to a wedding, but out in the surf or on the mountain you need something else."

What's so fascinating about this example is how different buyer personas articulate problems. Photographers said, "How can I protect my camera in the water?" But surfers asked, "How can I take photos while surfing?" Buyer persona research yields surprising information and leads to resonators; when you are tuned in to a problem people are willing to spend money to solve (in this example, shooting photos while performing an already difficult task) and you build a product that solves it, you are on the road to success. Don't believe that this product resonates with participants in one of the fastest-growing sports in the world? Then check out the showcase of user-submitted surf shots available on the company Web site.

Soon Woodman tuned in to buyer personas representing other extreme sports. "Because surfing is so demanding from a usability and environmental standpoint, our product also worked very well for other adventure sports," he says. For other sports, the core camera is the same, but the associated accessories and mount (the apparatus that affixes the camera) are different. For example, GoPro adapts to mount onto bicycle handlebars and onto helmets and various body parts for sports like rock climbing and kayaking. When adapting the camera to a new sport, Woodman has several prototypes built and then goes into the field to ask people to use the product, beat it up, and give feedback. "One of the great things about the markets we sell to is that they are made of passionate people," he says. "The things that we think of could never be thought of in a boardroom. Ideas come when we are out playing. We go straight to the source. We don't ask our grandmother what she thinks about our motor sport mounts apparatus; we ask race car drivers."

Chapter Summary

+ Tuned in organizations understand that the best way to develop products and services that resonate is to find unresolved problems for particular groups of people, groups called *buyer personas*.

+ Buyer personas are a tool you use to develop empathy with and a deep understanding of the real people whom you solve problems for, as opposed to a nameless, faceless "prospect."

+ By breaking down buyers into distinct groups, understanding what problems they have and how to solve them, and then cataloging everything you know about each buyer persona, you make it far easier to create breakthrough experiences, articulate powerful ideas about what your company can do, and establish connections with your customers.

+ This approach is utterly different from what most organizations do: either not segmenting the market at all (creating nonspecific offerings and marketing them to everyone), or segmenting based on their own egotistical view of the world.

+ For each buyer persona profile you create, you should develop a written document with as much information as you can gather about this group of people. What are your buyer personas' problems? Are they willing to pay money to solve these problems? What is the ideal product or service that can help them? How can we reach them? What media do they rely on for answers to problems?

+ Simply put, you want to know, in detail, the things that are important for each buyer persona. The best way to learn about buyers and develop buyer persona profiles is to interview people. We have no doubt that representatives of the two 2004 presidential candidates interviewed many NASCAR Dads, Security Moms, and other buyer personas they identified.

+ "To grok" is to have a deep, visceral understanding of your buyers.

✦ To grok a buyer persona means that you know as much about these buyers as they know about themselves.

✦ We encourage you to name your buyer personas.

✦ No buyer persona is ever complete. Your goal is to commit to an ongoing process where you continue to learn more and gain deeper insight into your buyer personas.

6

Step 3: Quantify the Impact

How do we know if we have a potential winner?

For probably as long as there have been tickets for sporting, concert, theater, and other live events, people have found themselves with extras they cannot use. And there have been countless other people prepared to pay for good seats when those are no longer available or even when the event is completely sold out. Until recently, the only option for buyers and sellers was to venture into the dark and murky world of ticket scalpers, who show up at popular events to hawk tickets. Seats for premier concerts like The Rolling Stones, Bruce Springsteen, and Hannah Montana, as well as National Football League and Major League Baseball games and international sporting events like the Olympic Games or World Cup soccer matches, often sell out quickly, leaving fans who wait until the last minute with nowhere else to turn. At the same time, those with extra tickets know that they have something of value but don't often have a convenient outlet for connecting with buyers.

StubHub identified this market problem in 2000 and quickly created the largest ticket market-place (by sales) in the world. StubHub offers fans an online marketplace to buy and sell tickets at fair market value. The problem of having or need-ing extra tickets is one that many fans have experi-enced, and it's quantifiable because the face value is right there on the ticket—if you've got two extra tickets to the Roger Waters con-cert and you paid a hundred bucks each for them, you've got a $200 unresolved problem and you're willing to act on it. It's also possible to quantify the extent of the problem for the person who is ready to buy tickets, because she has a price in mind that she's willing to pay to score those hard-to-find seats to a sold-out show.

Interestingly, StubHub also identified another kind of ticket aftermarket for shows that are not sold out—sellers who are willing to take a loss on their tickets just to get even a little cash back, and buyers who are thrilled to purchase seats for less than the box office price.

Understanding these distinct but complementary problems (sellers of tickets and buyers of tickets are two distinct buyer per-sonas), the StubHub online ticket marketplace created a break-through experience for fans, providing an easy way to buy or sell tickets in a safe, central, and reliable online environment. StubHub also partners directly with sports teams to help their fans get rid of extra tickets, thus alleviating some of the stigma of scalping, which has been illegal in some locations (although most U.S. states have relaxed such laws due to an overwhelming outcry by citizens). In August 2007, Major League Baseball and StubHub established a five-year deal for StubHub to become the official online provider of secondary tickets for MLB.com, the official Web site of Major League Baseball. As a part of the deal, StubHub also received offi-cial, club-endorsed status from each participating Major League Baseball team.[1]

By getting tuned in to the unresolved problems of tickets buyers and sellers, and quantifying the impact on consumers (as we'll teach you how to do in this chapter), StubHub created a breakthrough ex-perience that resonated. As a result, the company has enjoyed tremen-dous success. In early 2007, StubHub was acquired by eBay in a deal worth $310 million. And in October 2007, the company announced that it was quickly approaching its ten millionth ticket sale since its founding in late 2000. Considering it was less than a year earlier—November 2006—that StubHub hit its *five* millionth ticket milestone (with a sale of tickets for game two of the 2006 Major League Baseball World Series), this growth rate is amazing. This is the power of a resonator in the hands of a tuned in organization that understands the quantifiable size of its market.

Urgent, Pervasive, and Buyers Who Are Willing to Pay

There are three important criteria for you to consider as you measure the potential market for your product: (1) Is the problem urgent? (2) Is it pervasive in the market? (3) Are buyers willing to pay to have this problem solved? (And you also want to know how much the willing buyers are ready to pay, of course.) Quantifying this information is a critical and often overlooked step that you should perform *before* developing any products or services. Having the discipline to answer these questions will keep you from having to guess about whether a product can become a success.

Before you create a product or service, you must know that the problem you will solve is urgent and pervasive, and that buyers will be willing to spend money to solve it.

You need to run your ideas for a product or service through what we call the "urgent," "pervasive," and "willing-to-pay" filters. The answer to all three questions must be "yes" before you begin to create a product or service. If you encounter any negative answers, you should consider dropping the idea and move on to something else.

1. Is the Problem *Urgent?*

When you identify problems in the market, make sure that people really care about them. Are they actually urgent? We recognize that "urgent" is a powerful word and that you might doubt the need for this filter. But nothing is more frustrating than working yourself silly to solve a problem that either doesn't exist yet or that people describe as "not a big deal."

The ticket resale market that StubHub identified fits the "urgent filter." We've been on both the sell side and the buy side of the ticket resale market, and can confirm that when you want to see a show (or have a few hundred bucks worth of tickets you don't need), the problem becomes urgent (just ask any Stones diehard or parent of a Hannah Montana fan). If the event is in a few days, you've got to act; StubHub can help.

2. Is the Problem *Pervasive*?

You should identify a problem shared by a large enough number of people; otherwise it's not worthwhile for your organization to develop a product or service to solve it. Thus, it's important to use quantitative measurement to verify the commonality of the problem. How many people have this problem? Are there any unifying characteristics of the people who have the problem?

The ticket resale market that StubHub identified also fits the "pervasive filter." Every day there are countless sporting, music, theater, and other live events in thousands of cities and towns where people have extra tickets and others want to buy them.

3. Are People Willing to Pay to Solve the Problem?

Identify a problem that people are willing to pull money out of their pocket (or their companies' bank accounts) to solve. Tread carefully on this point, because most people have all kinds of problems that they're just not willing to pay money to solve. For example, you may hate going to the grocery store, but are you willing to pay someone else to purchase groceries for you? Apparently not that many people are, because many grocery delivery services have appeared in recent years and struggled to find enough buyers willing to pay for the service.

The ticket resale market that StubHub identified fits this third filter too. Sellers of tickets are happy to pay a small commission to StubHub in order to recoup some of the ticket price. At the same time, buyers are prepared to pay a premium to attend a sold-out show. And those looking to buy tickets to an event that has not sold out are willing to offer something less than face value, saving money from the price at the box office even after the commission.

First Urgent, Then Pervasive

Until now, the Tuned In Process we've shared with you has been qualitative—that is, we've described how to conduct research on market problems and interview buyer personas by getting out of your comfortable offices and actually talking to people. However, once you find a compelling problem that your organization can solve for buyers, you must switch to measuring and quantifying the potential buyer impact of your problem or service. This will help you determine if solving this problem for buyers is worth your company's effort. Quantifying the impact is the step that will help you build a business case for your new solution.

However, it's critical that you not simply skip to this step. We see many companies that short-circuit the process by creating an inside-out product (dreaming it up in a conference room instead of by going out and understanding buyer problems) and then apply measurement tools to validate the already tuned out idea. Don't fall into this trap!

The people behind StubHub discovered market problems first. That made the measurement step easy, because tickets have a well-defined face value. If you purchased a pair of tickets and cannot use them, you know exactly how much you'll lose unless you can sell them. Similarly, when people want to attend a sold-out show, the price of a coveted ticket typically starts at face value and goes up from there. It is also possible to quantify how many events occur in certain cities and how many typically sell out.

At this stage of the Tuned In Process, you can start to use measurement tools such as surveys. But remember, we never recommend using surveys to *find* unresolved problems. Remember the remote locator? If Magnavox had asked: "What problems does your TV have?" Very few people would have said: "I lose my remote." People often cannot identify problems for themselves. So to find unresolved problems like Magnavox did, you should always perform that step through in-person interviews.

There are a number of ways to measure the impact of solving a problem.

✦ Publicly available (and free) sources such as data from the U.S. Census or industry and trade associations.

✦ Specialist research reports that can be purchased "off the shelf" for a few hundred to several thousand dollars.

✦ Surveys that you conduct yourself or commission from a survey firm. These surveys can be conducted via telephone, in person, or by mail.

✦ Web-based surveys. If you have your own online contact list or a well-trafficked Web site, you may get people to respond to your request for information.

✦ Telemarketers may be a good resource. Using a telemarketing firm or your own people to measure is not sales. Instead, you call a bunch of people to see how many have the problem you've identified and then ask if they would pay to solve it.

Whoever Has the Best Data Wins

As we discussed in Chapter 2, many companies just guess when deciding what products and services to introduce to the market. But the Tuned In Process is a terrific way to stop the guesswork that goes on in so many organizations. We've witnessed the transformation that takes place when companies start to use the Tuned In Process, and many executives are amazed at the result.

Absent any real data, conference rooms are just full of opinions.

We love the hush that transfigures a conference room when an employee provides quantitative data showing how urgent and pervasive a newly identified problem is, and how much money people are willing to pay to solve it. That hush is usually followed by an excitement, since those present understand that the product development team can now jump right in and start developing a creative solution, using the company's distinctive competence. (We will elaborate on this process in Chapter 7.) If someone else in the conference room has a different idea, the group simply asks to see market data to support it. If there's no data, it's just an opinion, and is therefore irrelevant. We realize that this sounds harsh, and we also know it's not how most companies do it.

Data trumps opinion every time.

Tuned-In Impact-Continuum

Let's be realistic. Even though we advocate getting product ideas solely from buyers, we know there are times when an idea comes instead from the company founder, the CEO, someone in the product development department, a customer, or even—in certain circumstances—a competitor. And we know many employees sometimes feel an insurmountable pressure (or even a direct mandate) to proceed with such ideas against all common sense. (Remember the Susan B. Anthony dollar from Chapter 2?) The Tuned In Process's solution to this common occurrence is what we call an *Acid Test*. When you are being pressured to build an inside-out product, we suggest that you simply let the market decide whether it's a good idea. The Acid Test doesn't take long to prepare and need not be expensive.

First, you need some kind of prototype to show to buyers. It doesn't even need to be a completed product or service; you could just prepare a presentation (one like your salespeople would give) and use that to show what your organization plans to offer. Next, meet with potential buyers one at a time (not in a focus group situation). Don't tell them the benefits of your product or service—just show them what it does and ask them the following questions:

✦ What problems does it solve?
✦ How would they benefit from using it?
✦ What impact would it have on them, their families, or their companies?

Finally, you will plot where your new product or service idea fits on a spectrum we call the *Tuned-In Impact-Continuum*. For example, some people think getting the daily newspaper is a valuable part of their day. For others, newspaper subscriptions are no more than another daily chore: walking to the street to pick up the paper, later on tossing it into the waste can, usually unopened.

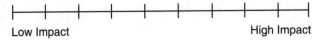

Low Impact   High Impact

The Tuned-In Impact-Continuum provides a simple method for buyers to plot existing and potential new offerings against each other to determine relative value from low impact to high impact.

On the far left of the continuum are products and services that have very little or no impact on your buyers' lives or jobs. On the far right, we plot products and services that represent a breakthrough. These products have a real and meaningful impact on buyers—like a medical advance that could save your life. Of course, most products lie somewhere in between, so you'll want to speak to a large enough sampling of buyers to accurately place your new product or service idea on the continuum.

This is not to say that low impact is always bad and high impact is necessarily good. Low-impact products—such as rubber bands—can be profitable. But you see lots of headlines about life-saving medical breakthroughs, not about the humdrum rubber band industry. Low-impact products, often considered commodities, march along quietly in a relatively stable market.

> **All that matters is your prospective customers' perceptions of the impact of your product on their lives, relationships, or jobs.**

Doing an Acid Test and plotting the results on the Tuned-In Impact-Continuum allow your organization to be realistic about a product or service's potential for success. The Acid Test helps you identify low-impact products before you invest heavily under the mistaken assumption that your product will be important to buyers. Because it doesn't matter what *you* think about the product or how much you have invested—all that matters is what your buyers think. On the other hand, high-impact products carry a significant risk because they are typically expensive and time-consuming to build. That is why an Acid Test is essential before the investment is made. If it is a bad product idea, the earlier you kill it, the better.

When you visit prospective buyers to perform the Acid Test on your as yet undeveloped product, draw the continuum on paper or a white board, and ask them to place on the chart some products and services that they already use. For example, if you sell a software product, ask them if they own Microsoft Word. If they say yes, ask them to point to where it fits on the Impact Continuum. Once they indicate the spot, your next question should be "Why did you choose that location?" Their answers will provide valuable information about what problems the product solves for this buyer.

Help them with one or two more products, and then ask them to name some products (that they already own) that are low impact and some that are high impact. At this stage, your buyers are likely to be enjoying this "game" and are happily plotting other products on the Impact Continuum. In each case, ask them why they placed each product where they did. Then, after you show them your prototype or sample, ask them where they would place *it* on the Impact Continuum. Many companies we've worked with have been shocked by what they find out. The "killer product" that you were sure everyone would love and value somehow winds up off to the left, exiled in low-impact territory by your buyers. On the other hand, we have seen very simple products—even ones that companies have given away for free—score very high on the Impact Continuum scale.

Solving Problems for Road Warriors

Research In Motion (RIM), the company behind the BlackBerry handheld communications device, identified a common problem: professionals who are frequently on the road couldn't keep up with e-mail and data from the home office. Internet technology had evolved to enable on-the-road connectivity, but unless you were in a hotel room that offered dial-up access, you had no way to stay connected to your valuable information. And dial-up service, the only option at the time, was painfully slow.

Initial buyer personas for the BlackBerry were professionals such as salespeople, individual consultants and financial services specialists (who might buy a unit to become more productive), and their department heads (who might buy a bunch of units for everyone on the team). Businesspeople who spend days or weeks away from the office need to know what's going on before meetings. Did anyone send me an important e-mail? Is there anything in the news? Did someone in the home office update important data? A mobile professional needs to answer all these questions, and if he or she can access the information immediately before meetings, they can stay in the data loop.

The problem RIM identified passed the urgent, pervasive, and willing-to-pay money filters. A businessperson is only as good as the information they deliver, so keeping up with the latest is certainly urgent. Millions of mobile professionals work in North America, so the problem is pervasive. And although the BlackBerry wasn't cheap upon launch (several hundred dollars to buy the unit, and a monthly fee to subscribe to the wireless data transmission service), many high-income individuals and team leaders were willing to pay to solve their communications problem with a BlackBerry.

The product was a tremendous success and continues to grow. As of April 2007, Blackberry service network had 8 million subscribers and Research in Motion has sold 6.4 million units in the current fiscal year.[2]

We've plotted the results of the Tuned-In Impact-Continuum for RIM as they were investigating market problems that eventually led to the Blackberry.

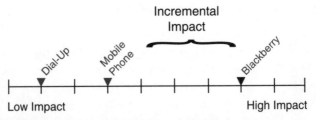

For mobile professionals seeking remote access to corporate information, the sizable incremental impact between using dial-up and cell phones and the BlackBerry signaled a potential resonator.

How Much Should We Charge?

The results of your Acid Test can help you with more than just making a decision about whether to move ahead with a product. One clever use of this process is that, once the potential customer has plotted a number of products (including yours!), you can go back and research the prices of the other products and get an indication of how you should price your new offering.

We know of one business-to-business software product that provided network administrators in large organizations with a seamless way of interfacing multiple operating environments. The utility took less than a day to build and cost nothing to replicate. The company's product development insiders wanted to give the product away, since it had only taken one day to develop. However, the product scored as very high impact with buyers on the Tuned-In Impact-Continuum scale. So the marketing people, armed with data from the Tuned-In Impact-Continuum scale, priced the product at $20,000. All the opinions of company insiders were proven wrong when the company began selling many copies of the software.

> **The Acid Test and the Impact Continuum identified a product that insiders wanted to give away but that instead became a highly profitable resonator.**

In another example, a colleague had planned to charge $12,000 for a business product, but buyers rated it much higher on the Tuned-In Impact-Continuum scale, so they changed the selling price to $72,000. In another case, a product everyone inside the company thought would be a clear winner scored very low on the Tuned-In Impact-Continuum scale, so it was never produced, probably saving the company a great deal of money and resources.

The Acid Test and Your Buyer Personas

When you conduct your Acid Test, remember that representatives of diverse buyer personas will rate the same product and service in dramatically different ways. The more you solicit input from potential buyers, the better your data. For example, bank presidents might rate the *Wall Street Journal* as high-impact, but truck drivers typically don't. By asking both groups why, you learn what problems the product solves for buyers who rate it as high-impact. You can then communicate to other potential buyers in the same market segment that you have solved those high-impact problems.

Even products that were created using the Tuned In Process should be run through the Acid Test. Although you will already know that the problems you're trying to solve are urgent, pervasive, and worth spending money on, an Acid Test helps you confirm that you actually solved the entire problem. The worst scenario for a tuned in product is that you provided only a partial solution to the problem you identified. Obviously, most buyers don't want a partial solution, so they'll be unlikely to buy it. More importantly, though, by going to market with a compelling but only partially solved problem, you open the door for more agile competitors to come in with the complete solution.

Developing a Tuned In Business Proposal

Congratulations! If you've read this far, we thank you for sticking with us. If you're beginning to apply the Tuned In Process to your own business, now is the time that you create a brief written proposal to help you articulate your idea for a product or service to your constituents.

The proposal is the tool you'll use to succinctly articulate your product or service. You can use the proposal with internal audiences such as the product development team, your spouse, and salespeople. And it can also be used as a tool to help communicate your ideas to potential investors, business partners, and others with a stake in your idea.

We suggest that a simple one- or two-page business proposal, one that encapsulates the essence of the product or service you want to create, is all you need. Your short proposal should include the details of what you've learned so far in the Tuned In Process: your targets and strategy, the operating details, and how you will make money from the product or service. It doesn't have to be any more complicated than that.

Your proposal should answer the following questions:

+ What detailed unresolved problems are you solving?
+ Who will your solution impact (what buyer personas) and how many such people are there?
+ What product or service will you create to solve the problem?
+ How does your product or service impact buyers?
+ How will buyers quantify that value?
+ What will it take to convert prospects into customers?

A tuned in business proposal will help you make "go/no-go" and "buy versus build" decisions.

While we recognize that there are countless other details that can (and often do!) go into these documents, answering the questions above in as simple and straightforward a way as possible will help your decision makers determine a course of action. Above all, remember that your most important task is capturing the essence of how you (or your business) are going solve problems in the marketplace.

Measure What Matters

Measurements of business success (or lack of it) are a tricky matter for many companies. Among the leaders we've interviewed in the past ten years, the ones who were successful made sure to measure only what was important to run their businesses; they avoided or ignored the distracting data that often flood executives. Tuned in organizations don't fall prey to the typical requests for minutia that come from investors, boards, and analysts. Their leaders recognize the disease that leads to death by metrics. Of course, nobody would argue that data and metrics have no value, particularly when these numbers provide transparency into company performance.

The problem with measurement is that too many companies have trained their employees to measure the wrong things.

Many managers are required to deliver detailed metrics on such things as the number and type of sales leads (sometimes on a daily basis), the number of "PR hits" (magazine and newspaper articles mentioning the company), the number of visitors to each of the company's Web pages, engineering productivity rates, regional sales performance, and this, and that, and more. Well, guess what? Those numbers don't matter. They only serve to create an environment where people work hard but not smart. Measuring the wrong things (such as Web hits, press clips, and the like) leads to tuned out behavior.

Instead, you should measure how many meetings with buyers you and your team are conducting. How often do you get out of the office and meet with actual people to learn about their problems? Measure the impact of solving the problems you've identified. Measure how your different buyer personas learn about new ways to solve their problems. And, once your product or service is out on the market, you should measure how well it resonates with each of your buyer personas.

In short, when creating a tuned in product experience, recognize that you should only measure what matters. Measurement will serve as the dashboard for how you run the organization and will help to answer questions: Should you spend money to create a new product or service? Should you expand your marketing programs to reach a new buyer persona? Should you develop a new channel to reach the European market?

Tuned in leaders keep track of the meaningful information they need to drive the business forward, not a bunch of trumped-up data used to justify employees' tuned out work.

Tuned In . . . without a Credit Card

According to Forrester Research, one-third of Web users refuse to use credit cards online, a huge issue for people who sell goods and services or solicit money over the Internet.[3] Gary Marino knew about this problem with doing business online because he had worked as chief credit officer at Citibank for fifteen years and ran credit and marketing operations at First USA. Thus, he founded a new company, Bill Me Later, to solve this market problem. His company learned that people were concerned that their personal credit card information would be stolen. Although the industry reports that less than 1 percent of credit card fraud is associated with interception of credit card numbers through online shopping, buyers perceived it as a real problem. Bill Me Later also learned that, oftentimes, a customer might not have access to the credit card number at the time of the transaction (for instance, if his or her wallet wasn't nearby). And a large market segment chose not to carry a card at all, despite having good credit scores.

In 2002, Bill Me Later set out to introduce a new credit vehicle for consumers—a daunting challenge given that many big banks (such as Marino's former employers) had tried to and largely failed. The last resonator developed by the industry had been the Discover Card, launched at great expense over twenty years earlier.

To use the Bill Me Later payment service, online consumers simply enter their birth date and the last four digits of their social security number. Bill Me Later can then, through their patented process, instantly approve the credit account. The company then follows up two weeks later by mail with a bill for the purchase. The consumer then has the choice of paying it off interest free or making payments over time, just like a credit card. This process solves serious problems for those who don't carry a card and those who are concerned about Internet security. At the same time, online merchants who made Bill Me Later one of their payment options generated more sales.

In fact, Bill Me Later conducted buyer persona research with the merchants to learn about their market problems too. They discovered merchants were paying 2 percent or more in fees to credit card companies, so Bill Me Later offered their service for 1.5 percent, knowing that every percentage point was important to margin-conscious online retailers. Another problem these merchants faced was high abandonment rates for virtual shopping carts (people sometimes shop online, put stuff in their "baskets," and then mysteriously go away). The new Bill Me Later payment option dramatically reduced the abandonment rate, and merchants even said that Bill Me Later clients were shopping more often and spending as much as 250 percent more than comparable credit card customers.

Bill Me Later became a resonator for both merchants and online shoppers. The company has signed up hundreds of merchants, including Wal-Mart, PETCO, Overstock.com, Continental Airlines, SkyMall, JetBlue, Hotels.com, and 49 of the other 200 top online retailers.

And because of initial success, the company garnered $100 million in venture capital funding. As of 2007, after only five years, Bill Me Later had rocketed to number six on the Inc. 5000, *Inc.* magazine's list of the fastest-growing privately held companies in America. They reported growing from $613,000 in revenue in 2003 to $53.6 million in 2006 with transaction volume in excess of $1 billion—with only 100 employees.

By getting tuned in to customer problems, merchant problems, and even investor problems, and then quantifying their impact, Bill Me Later was able to create the perfect solution for each party. We hope that by studying the stories throughout this book, you've also learned how to create a resonator of your own.

Chapter Summary

+ Once you find a compelling problem that your organization can solve, you must switch to measuring and quantifying the impact on buyers.
+ Measurement will help you determine if solving this problem for buyers is worth the effort for your company.
+ There are three important criteria for you to consider as you measure: (1) Is the problem urgent? (2) Is it pervasive in the market? (3) Are buyers willing to pay to have this problem solved?
+ Quantifying the impact of the problem will provide the data you need to build a business case.
+ A simple one- or two-page tuned in business proposal encapsulates the essence of the product or service that you want to build and will help you make "go/no-go" and "buy versus build" decisions.
+ Measurement will serve as the dashboard for how you run the organization—that is, how you go about the business of solving your customers' problems. Thus, you should only measure what matters and not get bogged down by meaningless corporate data like Web site hits and productivity rates.

7

 # Step 4: Create Breakthrough Experiences

How do we build a competitive advantage?

I magine you want to start a new church. What do you do? Well, you might look for (or commission) a building, buy some stained glass and an organ, and hire a pastor, right? Not necessarily. If you're tuned in, you'll realize that there are far different things you should be doing to establish a church that resonates with parishioners. In any marketplace (even a ministry) following the Tuned In Process is a proven way to create success. Start by understanding the problems that potential churchgoers have, the different types of people who might attend church, and the compelling reasons why people go to church to begin with.

Mark Batterson is the lead pastor of a hugely popular church in the Washington, DC, metropolitan area. But his isn't a typical church, because he doesn't actually have a church building, or traditional services, or many of the other usual symbols of religious devotion. Instead Batterson tuned in to his market: the tens of thousands of twentysomethings who had largely ignored other churches in the area. Batterson learned that a church building can be an obstacle for many young people, so his National Community Church (also known as Theater-Church.com) conducts five services per week in three nontraditional locations—for example, movie theaters on Sunday mornings, when they aren't being used for movies.[1] And because most of his "buyers" don't drive, the locations are all near subway stops.

National Community Church makes extensive use of audiovisual and Internet technology to tell stories and build a spiritual community both on- and offline. At the National Community Church studio, Batterson and his staff develop video stories that add color and flavor to the live services. "I think that church should be the most creative place on the planet," Batterson says. "The medieval church had stained glass to tell the gospel story to the churchgoers, who were mostly illiterate. We use the movie studio to tell the story to people. We use video to add color and to add flavor to what we do. If Jesus had video in his day, it wouldn't surprise me if he made short films."

TheaterChurch.com includes a content-rich Web site, podcasts of the weekly services (audio content delivered by subscription to people's computers and iPods), and a motivational "Spirit Fuel" Webcast series. Each one of these initiatives is the result of understanding the needs of young people who want a church home that speaks directly to their needs and uses the technologies they're familiar with.

Batterson also writes an extremely popular blog and has used it to gain online fame well beyond the Washington, DC, area—his blog is followed by tens of thousands of readers all over the world, and the podcast is one of the fastest-growing church podcasts in America. The tuned in approach of understanding buyers (in this case, the people that Batterson wants to attract to church) has been wildly successful. Weekend attendance at National Community

Church exceeds 1,000 adults in an average weekend; 70 percent of them are single people in their twenties. Clearly, National Community Church is a resonator.

As Batterson has shown, the best way to succeed in any market is by being tuned in. Even when developing a new church, the best approach is to understand market problems, identify buyer personas, and then build an experience that resonates. In this chapter, we'll talk about that last step.

Experiences That Resonate

As you develop product and service experiences, remember that word we keep using—*experience*. There is much more to your product or service than most companies realize. The most successful organizations understand that customers buy a total experience, and so they do their best to create one that resonates. There are five common parts of the buyer experience that people care about:

Breakthrough experiences incorporate each experience—from the first interaction through evaluation, purchase, product use, and after-sale service.

✦ **The discovery experience.** Buyers need information to make rational and informed decisions about how to solve their problems. Tuned in organizations create marketing materials that people actually *want* to consume, while tuned out companies focus on hype and spin in a misguided attempt to manipulate minds. A tuned in company, for example, might run a blog where real people in the organization could let the public see how they went about problem solving. In the long run, leaders will benefit greatly when they integrate marketing experiences that are simple, nonthreatening, and—above all—useful.

✦ **The buying experience.** What makes some products easy to buy while others are an uncomfortable hassle? The tuned out company just wants to make orders easy for the company to process, not easy or fun for buyers to place. Buyers want to feel important, and they want their needs to be met throughout the sales process. It doesn't matter if you're selling a five-dollar deli sandwich or a thirty-thousand-dollar boat, making the buying experience as simple and pleasurable as possible will lead to more sales.

✦ **The packaging experience.** A very popular corporate gift in Japan is beautifully packaged fruit. The boxes are exquisite, with textured tissue papers cradling each perfectly ripe melon, apple, or pear (hand-selected, naturally, to be the perfect shape, size, and color). The fantastic packaging allows the fruit boxes to sell for sometimes more than ten times the price of the fruit itself. On the other hand, other buyer personas appreciate a minimalist approach to packaging and prefer to buy fruit in bulk to save money. Our colleague was in the grocery store recently as a man and his kindergarten-age daughter wheeled up alongside her in the produce department. As the dad bagged apples, the little girl reached for cleverly packaged cherry tomatoes (yellow-bottomed container with a domed lid). To a child, this does seem rather like a "toy." The little girl grabbed one and said, "Daddy, can we get these?" Wow. A kid wanted to buy cherry tomatoes! She was old enough to know what they were, but too young to realize that they are just the same old cherry tomatoes normally sold in pint containers.

+ **The "using" experience.** Breakthrough experiences are simple to understand and implement. They are intuitive and natural and help people engage with the product or service. For example, when one of us recently dropped our car off at the dealer for repair, we were given a loaner car. To our amazement, the dealership had tuned the radio station in the loaner to the same station we had on in the car we dropped off. Simple improvements such as this one, which probably takes less than a minute to implement, can make huge differences to people.

+ **The service experience.** Many products and services need to come with some form of after-sale customer care. Tuned out organizations outsource this function to uninformed third parties to save costs, or they might even eliminate the function entirely and leave customers on their own. But tuned in companies understand that happy customers will talk about their positive service experiences with friends and family (or on blogs and forums), and possibly purchase more of your products and services themselves. At the Pragmatic Marketing offices, we have a BUNN automatic coffee maker. We recently noticed that the coffee maker was dripping, so we called the 800 number for service and described the problem over the phone. Within an hour, the service person was onsite and fixed the problem. This remarkable experience had our office abuzz with amazement. Guess where we'll be buying our next coffeemaker?

Your breakthrough experience is likely to include each of these five areas, but you may end up focusing on several. Your choice of how to focus will be based on your distinctive competence.

Engineering a Breakthrough Experience

As we discussed in Chapter 2, innovation based on raw creativity, whimsy, or guesswork is unlikely to create breakthrough experiences. While it is possible to create a (successful) innovative product or service in the vacuum of your insular company conference rooms, that process of guessing is much more risky than getting tuned in to your market. And as we discussed in Chapter 5, the best way to get tuned in to your market is to learn about your buyers' problems through in-depth interviews. Next, we'll discuss how to use that interview data to identify the attributes of a breakthrough product or service and create a resonator. First, let's look at an example.

For the past decade, Boeing and Airbus have been locked in a two-way battle in the large passenger-aircraft market. A $150 million manufactured product doesn't seem to fit the classic definition of a "commodity," but nevertheless the commercial aircraft market has essentially become a commodity market in recent years. The only real differentiation between products has been in price: what deal an airline could negotiate with the companies.

Executives at Boeing want to change those market dynamics. To create the new 250-passenger 787 Dreamliner, Boeing not only tuned in to the product's buyers (airlines), but also and especially the buyer's customers (millions of people who fly regularly).[2] Boeing created an executive-level position charged with leading the effort, naming Blake Emery the director of differentiation strategy for the company. Emery and his team met with members of several buyer personas, passengers as well as airline professionals—pilots, cabin crew, and mechanics. This approach (particularly the focus on passengers) was a radical departure from the typical focus of dealing with aircraft purchasing managers, who tend to care only about the bottom line and cutting the best deal. The research led to such innovations as the use of carbon fiber in the wings and fuselage, which, combined with more efficient engines, will cut fuel consumption. (Carbon fiber also requires less maintenance than aluminum.)

However, the biggest innovations came from detailed discussions the differentiation team had with multiple groups of airline passengers from different countries. The team wanted to find out what people from many different cultures really wanted from an airliner (besides the usual request for more legroom). A major finding of this buyer persona research was that passengers felt increasingly confined and restricted as they walked down the boarding bridge and into the airplane.

The Boeing team used the information from the passenger meetings to guide the design of a cabin interior that creates the sense of being in a much larger, more welcoming space. The ceiling lighting is washed with hidden lights that draw the eyes upward and create a sense of infinity (in sharp contrast to the cramped feeling generated by the fluorescent-tube lighting used in existing aircraft cabins). Flight attendants can change the brightness and color of the cabin lighting to create a sense of morning, dusk, and nighttime, minimizing the disorienting effects of life across time zones. Luggage bins in the Dreamliner aren't just larger than in other aircraft; they're also curved and placed flatter against the ceiling to keep from banging passengers' heads.

"Flying is a magical way to travel, says Emery. "What we're trying to do with the Dreamliner is bring back a little of that magic we lost along the way."

Boeing is taking these passenger-driven enhancements and using them to sell a new idea: that passengers will actually book with an airline that flies the new Dreamliner because they expect to have a better experience on that plane. As frequent travelers on the business speaking circuit, we can relate. We often shun small, commuter-style aircraft because they are less comfortable. So far, airlines seem to agree. As of this writing, forty-seven customers worldwide have ordered 677 airplanes worth more than $110 billion at current list prices. The first 787 is scheduled to enter passenger service in 2009.

Products and Services That Resonate

Let's revisit the idea of products and services that resonate. Think back on the ones we've discussed so far. The hotel at the end of the train line resonates with the sleepy Japanese salaryman who missed his stop. The GoPro camera resonates with surfers because they can carry it on their wrist. Zipcar resonates with people who occasionally need a set of wheels for a quick run to Costco. And National Community Church resonates with twentysomethings who want a spiritual home that fits their lifestyle. What do all of these ideas have in common? Each one is a breakthrough product or service that buyers immediately understand has value to them, even if they have never heard of the company or its products before. They're all *resonators*.

As we noted in Chapter 1, the Apple iPod is a great example of a resonator. The problem that the iPod solved was not simply the need for a better MP3 player, although that's the form the solution took. The real problem the iPod solved was that it used to be a pain to listen to digital music, especially on the go. But the iPod (with the help of iTunes) makes it easy to access songs and upload them to the device, and its elegant design emphasizes simplicity, so there is little need for instruction manuals and documentation. Most people who struggled through the awful rigmarole needed to get an older-generation MP3 player up and running heard about the iPod and immediately said, "Wow that sounds so much easier than all the work I had to do!" And millions more who had never gone through the trouble realized equally quickly that now they wouldn't have to.

The easiest way to create a breakthrough product or service is to follow the Tuned In Process; these steps will help you discover, create, and launch your own resonator.

Your Distinctive Competence

Buyers choose to purchase your product or service based on their belief that you provide something that solves their problems better than anyone else can. What are your organization's unique abilities to deliver value to your customers? We call these abilities your *distinctive competence*. Without identifying your distinctive competence, you'll be unable to differentiate your products and services from the pack. Building products and services based on your distinctive competence allows you to win even against larger, better funded, and more entrenched competitors.

Don't confuse distinctive competence with "core competency," a term many business people are familiar with. Your core competency is simply what your organization is good at. Distinctive competence is what you excel at *that your competitors do not*. Your distinctive competence is a subset of your core competency. For example, FedEx has many core competencies, including deep understanding of distribution technologies, aircraft operations (they run an air force–sized fleet, one of the largest in the world), and Web site robustness (they are regularly one of the top thousand most trafficked sites on the

Web). But with all those core competencies, the one thing FedEx focuses on as their distinctive competence is *reliability*. Every decision that the leaders at FedEx make supports the company's ability to provide and sustain a reliable package-delivery service.

What is your organization's distinctive competence?

Every company should be able to answer this question. If you can't yet, you should figure it out. Now. *Before* you get to work creating products and services.

The list here will give you an idea.[3] Your distinctive competence could be one of the following:

+ **An important feature.** Volvo has built a solid leadership position in a crowded automobile market by focusing on safety.
+ **Another possibility is ergonomics.** When we give presentations in front of large groups, we always use the Interlink RemotePoint Navigator because it has only four buttons—slide forward, slide back, slide hide, and a laser pointer. That's it. The other remotes cram in so many useless features that it's hard to avoid making mistakes—a serious problem when you're talking in front of five hundred people!
+ **A distinctive business model.** Perhaps your streamlined manufacturing and distribution capabilities allow you to sell products at a lower cost than any of your competitors can. Zipcar rents cars online, not in person like the other rental car companies do.
+ **A deep understanding of one particular buyer persona.** Cityside Garage in the Boston area only works on vintage Land Rovers and has a devoted following of enthusiasts who travel from all over New England to have their Land Rovers serviced.

These are just some examples of distinctive competence; the list certainly isn't comprehensive. In fact, your organization's distinctive competence could be virtually anything that helps you create break-through experiences. Your distinctive competence should *dictate* how you build products and services. Your product development department must build your distinctive competence into the product design. For example, if Volvo were to build a new sports car, the design team and R&D people would need to go about their work with the stated understanding that they were building "the safe sports car."

Highlighting your distinctive competence also helps describe your organization to buyers, so they are more likely to choose you instead of your competitor. Your distinctive competence drives your marketing communications initiatives because you use it to create connections with your buyers based on the products and services that your organization uniquely provides.

Mark Batterson at National Community Church has leveraged his distinctive competence by applying technology to church. Technology is so important to the church's activities that as of this writing, their leadership team includes a "media pastor" (Dave Clark), a "digital pastor" (David Russell), and a "buzz coordinator" (Juliet Main). Each of these professionals leverages his or her technological expertise to create a church experience that resonates with their market. Like Batterson, Clark and Russell also write blogs to stay connected to their audience. It may seem surprising (ironic even) for a church to have this particular distinctive competence, *but that's exactly why National Community Church is so successful.* How many churches in *your* neighborhood have a podcast? If one did, might you want to check it out? Might your college-age children want to check it out?

Understanding your own distinctive competence tells you what parts of your business to focus on—and what to outsource to others. Do you haul your own trash to the dump? Probably not, unless you're in the trash business. And why should you? It's better to focus on your distinctive competence and outsource much of the rest. Do you process your own payroll? Why? It's probably not your distinctive competence. But it *is* the distinctive competence of the payroll-processing companies; they're the ones with the skills and the experience. We encourage you to consider what parts of your business you're squandering management attention on. Can you free up valuable company time to better leverage your distinctive competence?

Make time to get together with your team and answer this important question: "What is our distinctive competence?" It will tell you what business functions to own and which to outsource, which meetings to attend and which to ignore, which products to build and which to buy.

The Ultimate Ice Cream Experience

When Doug Ducey took over as president of Cold Stone Creamery in 1995, he didn't worry about the 5,500 Dairy Queen or 4,400 Baskin-Robbins, or 3,300 TCBY franchises that many said were his biggest competition.[4] Nor did he obsess about the fact that 90 percent of ice cream sold in the United States was bought in retail grocery stores, where new entries had no access to shelf space. Instead, Ducey drew on his experience working as a brand manager for the Folgers product line at Procter & Gamble. He remembered how an upstart company from Seattle called Starbucks was able to create a breakthrough product experience in the coffee category. Now he saw a $21 billion ice cream industry that focused on producing tired, uninspired products—the Folgers coffee of desserts, essentially. He had ideas about how to change the game.

Instead of focusing, like other players in the market, on improving manufacturing or driving down costs, Cold Stone set out to improve customers' ice cream experience. By spending a great deal of time in Cold Stone stores watching how customers reacted to the variety of choices, and by starting every day listening and responding to customers on the company support line, Ducey identified a fundamental truth about going out for ice cream, one that the other guys were missing.

Ice cream makers are in the business of making people happy.

Going out for ice cream is an event. It's an indulgence that requires discretionary time and money. Most importantly, it's a *group* event, a shared experience between friends and family. Cold Stone developed an understanding of ice-cream buyer personas in order to identify and create what they call "the ultimate ice cream experience." Cold Stone ignored the competition and focused on what made people happy, including:

+ A clean, pleasant atmosphere with bright colors
+ Upbeat "crew members" who treat work as fun
+ Ice cream made fresh every day, with a wide variety to choose from
+ The ability to add "mix-ins" to customize the ice cream with multiple flavors and toppings
+ The chance to watch this personalized treat being prepared—mixed together on a cold granite stone

Cold Stone is built around the ice cream experience. If you walked into a Cold Stone store right now, you'd see siblings playfully arguing about the best combination of toppings. You'd see friends passing their creations around the table. You might even hear the employees behind the counter break out in song when they receive a tip. And you'd hear satisfied customers talking on their way out the door about what they want to try next time they go out for ice cream at Cold Stone.

Not surprisingly, this tuned in company is growing quickly. With almost 1,400 franchises now in operation, Cold Stone Creamery is the sixth best-selling brand of ice cream in the United States, and they operate stores in South Korea, Japan, Puerto Rico, and Taiwan.

Chapter Summary

+ Your organization's unique ability to offer superior value to your customers is called your *distinctive competence.*

+ Building products and services based on your distinctive competence allows you to win, even against larger, better funded, and more entrenched competitors.

+ Distinctive competence not only dictates how you build products and services, it also forms your marketing communications strategy and helps you describe your organization to buyers so they are more likely to choose you instead of your competitor.

+ Creating products and services based on your distinctive competence is the best way to develop a breakthrough experience.

+ The most successful organizations understand that people are buying a total experience, and they create one that resonates.

+ Five important parts of the buyer experience are the discovery experience, the buying experience, the packaging experience, the using experience, and the service experience.

CHAPTER

8

Step 5: Articulate Powerful Ideas

How do we establish memorable concepts that speak to the problems buyers have?

A colleague recently went through the process of designing and building a custom home. We had heard stories about how unpleasant that experience can be—skyrocketing costs, unmet promises, construction delays, and daily frustrations—so imagine our surprise when our colleague said his "dream home" exceeded all expectations and that the entire process was a pleasure! Wow. We had to learn more.

The first step in building a custom home is always design. The choice of architect is one of the earliest and most critical decisions. Our colleague could afford the best, so he initially arranged informational interviews with two of the area's leading architects. One was an award winner who had graced the covers of several designer-home magazines, and the other was a less well-known architect who had been recommended by a friend.

The first interview was with the famous architect, whom our colleague dubbed "the rock star." He showed up late for the appointment. When he finally breezed in with no words of apology, he focused attention on the large portfolio of work he had done for other customers. The rock star recommended options for our colleague's home that *he* thought would be really unique and that *he'd* like to explore. He then proceeded to sketch what he referred to as "next year's award-winning design." While our colleague was impressed with the work, he was interested to hear from the other candidate before taking anything to the next step.

The second interview with a lesser-credentialed architect began on time. When the two sat down, our colleague was expecting the same approach; he figured the architect would focus on his design portfolio.

Instead, the second architect just smiled and said, "Tell me how you live."

Our colleague immediately relaxed and started talking about his family's lifestyle. They spoke for several hours that first day, discussing such things as what the family does at home, how the parents interact with the kids, what they like (and dislike) about their current home, how often they entertain, and what their best experiences in their previous homes had been.

Our colleague said the choice for him was obvious from the moment the less famous architect said, "Tell me how you live." This question articulated a powerful idea: the client's problems, not the architect's ego, should come first. Needless to say, this idea resonated with our colleague.

After additional meetings to further discuss the family's lifestyle and to refine some early ideas, our colleague was thrilled with a home design that was perfect for him and his family. Ever since the build was completed (on time and on budget), his new home has been a place for his family to live the way they always wanted to, with surroundings designed to fit them and not the other way around.

Concepts That Resonate

If you've been following the Tuned In Process from the start, the step that we're discussing now—articulating powerful ideas—should be easy! After all, you've already spent a great deal of time understanding the unresolved market problems of your buyer personas. You've identified what's likely to resonate with your market, and you've built your product or service to deliver a breakthrough experience. If you've done those things right, then all you need to do next is focus on crafting those golden nuggets that will perfectly sum up what your organization does for your customers. You will want to express those morsels as one or more powerful ideas— phrases and concepts that resonate with your buyers.

The most powerful ideas are those that draw on your company's distinctive competence and map perfectly onto the unresolved problems of your buyer personas. For example, in just one phrase, "tell me how you live," our colleague's architect captures the needs of someone who is in the market to build a custom home. But the phrase also reflects the second architect's distinctive competence: designing houses perfectly suited to individual family's lifestyles. Finally, the phrase draws a sharp line between the second architect and his more famous competitor, the one who only cares about awards.

Powerful stuff.

What do you want your buyers to believe?

A remarkable thing about the most successful ideas of this kind is that they rarely have anything to do with describing what a product or service actually does. Instead, the most powerful ideas are used to express to each of your buyer personas what you want them to *believe* about your organization. Consider the 2004 U.S. presidential election again. You will recall from Chapter 5 that the campaigns identified buyer personas such as "NASCAR Dads" and "Security Moms." Armed with detailed information of these groups' problems, the campaigns created a set of powerful ideas to use during speeches, in position papers, TV ads, and direct mailings, and on Web sites. For example, George W. Bush consistently used the powerful phrase "Stay the Course" in speeches and advertising. This idea particularly appealed to Security Moms, highlighting the idea that their families would be safer from the threats of terrorism if Bush returned to office for another term instead of John Kerry. Interestingly, as we write this, we're in the thick of the presidential primary race in 2008, and many of those same Security Moms from 2004 are wondering if the Iraq war has gone on too long. As of this writing, the presidential candidates are struggling to articulate the particular ideas that resonate with voters who are part of this buyer persona.

You must draw from your work in the first steps of the Tuned In Process to express the powerful ideas that will resonate. What do you want each buyer persona to believe about your organization? What phrases will you use and how? Remember, people are buying *from your organization*, so how can you best articulate what's important about you? What else, besides just a product, is each buyer persona really looking for? Is it reliability (as with FedEx)? Luxury? The "safe choice?" Remember, Volvo doesn't just sell a car; it sells safety.[2]

Find What's Most Compelling

While the process of identifying the powerful ideas that will resonate with buyers is straightforward, it does require that you meet with them to learn about their problems (as we discussed in Chapter 4). This process takes time. We suggest that you meet with as many buyers as it takes to get answers that converge around both a common problem and a way to articulate the ideal solution that your company will deliver. How many meetings is that? It might take ten meetings with representatives of your buyer persona, or even twenty or more.

Then you need to turn these concepts into a powerful idea. This process isn't difficult either, but many people try to skip most of it and jump to the end. Or they try to reverse engineer the process by thinking up words in their own offices without meeting with buyers at all, merely guessing what the buyers would have said. Other people come up with a concept for a new product or service and then try to create a catchy slogan by hiring an expensive agency to "make it sexy"—again, all without speaking with a single buyer. These attempts often lead to disappointing results, because the manufactured ideas don't resonate with the buyers.

Instead, companies are left with meaningless slogans like "An Army of One." This slogan was used in recruitment efforts by the U.S. Army. Even if you understood that the slogan was trying to say that with today's technology a soldier can equal an army (playing up the screens and panels that make warfare look like playing video games), the message fell apart when a real war started with scenes of miserable living conditions and burning Humvees.[3] Rather than trying to develop a powerful idea through inside-out thinking via a committee, we follow these four steps:

1. Affinity mapping. You've already documented the problems your buyers experience. Hopefully, you've uncovered many detailed and specific problems, because your ideas need to be specific. If your offering saves your buyers money, don't just express the problem with the phrase "I need to save money." Dig deeper. Document the small problems you can solve that will capture the money. The more buyers you interview, the longer the list will be. The best lists include dozens of problems that you can solve. For example, Zipcar tackles problems such as "I don't want to secure or pay for car insurance" and "I don't want to locate and pay for a downtown parking spot" and "I don't need a car most of the time so why should I have to pay for one?"

Once you have documented the problems, you will notice some commonalities among them. Sort these into categories of similar problems, perhaps four or five. You then want to name the groups that you've identified. What you're looking for now is convergence around an idea (or ideas) you can use. For Zipcar, the three problems listed above could all be grouped as economic. Yet some of the same problems could also reside in other groups, such as convenience or the environment. Remember, what makes this process different from normal in-house brainstorming is that you're using real information you've gathered from your buyers, just as we did in Chapter 4.

2. The elevator speech. Once you have mapped and named the groups, you move to the second step—distilling the essence of the message about these groups of problems into a sentence or two, for about twenty-five words total. Many people refer to a statement like this as an "elevator speech." It's the answer you'd give if you were asked about what your company's product or service does but you only had seconds inside an elevator to do it.

The best elevator speeches are in the buyers' words, not your own egocentric corporate gobbledygook, so it is essential that you complete your affinity map before you develop the elevator speech. Otherwise, you will be tempted to talk about your product's features or about why your company is better than the competition. The elevator speech is all about buyers and the problems that your product or service will solve for them.

If your company sells a sales-force management system and you are speaking to a sales representative, your elevator speech might say, "Our product lets you do what you do best—show up on time, carry the right materials, sell, get your boss off your back, and eliminate your reporting nightmare."

3. The Acid Test. You started with specific problems collected from buyers, so your message will likely resonate. But, to be sure, conduct a quick acid test. Locate some people who represent the buyer persona you are selling to and run your elevator speech by them. Then ask the following types of questions:

+ Does this explanation make sense to you?
+ What does this product or service do?
+ If you heard this, would you be interested?
+ Would you want to buy or at least move along to the next step of the sales cycle?

Once the message passes the test, you know you have a very valuable tool. Your elevator speech should become an important component within all of your marketing materials, including your Web site, brochures, and press releases. You or your salesperson should also use that concise message to answer the question "Why should I buy your product?"

4. Refining the resonator. The elevator speech is your starting point for developing a powerful idea. The final step is to distill it into a hard-hitting and memorable concept. For Lexus automobiles, "The relentless pursuit of perfection." For Miller Lite, "Tastes great, less filling." For Bounty paper towels, "The quicker picker-upper," and for Burger King, "Have it your way." All these ideas are more than catchphrases; they're rooted in a set of problems that these products solve for buyers.

"The Elevator Speech Is Our Company's Compass"

When Mike Volpe joined HubSpot as vice president of marketing, he was the fourth employee at the Web-based marketing platform-provider for small and medium businesses, and its product was just being launched.[4] One of the first projects he embarked on was creating a new elevator speech to succinctly articulate what HubSpot does. "I was lucky that before I had fixed ideas in my head, I could talk to many people about what we do, and have lots and lots of conversations about what our buyers' problems are," Volpe says. He called people on the company's in-house contact lists and met others in person at industry events such as the MarketingSherpa Summit and on sites such as the Marketing Profs and LinkedIn. "I would say things like 'Tell me about your biggest challenges' or 'Have you done any search engine marketing?' " Volpe says. "We also asked people what words they would use to describe the solution to the problems they had."

Volpe made sure to keep an open mind as he went through the process. "We weren't sure how people would describe their problems," he says. "Then we brought all the things that we heard from about seventy-five individual discussions back to the office and we had an internal debate. We had to do internal soul searching because sometimes we'd hear things from four or five people that wouldn't work for others. And we heard things that were surprising. But the key to the process was that we started from what buyers said, not our own stuff."

Volpe ended up with eight candidates for his elevator speech. "They used similar words, so we bounced the ideas by some trusted advisers to choose the best one, and now we're implementing it," he says.

HubSpot is an inbound marketing system that uses the Internet to turn your company into a central hub for your market, so you get found by more prospects and convert higher percentages of them into paying customers.

Volpe says that all new customers are interviewed to find out why they made the purchase decision, and those reasons are mapped against the elevator speech. He also analyzes people who respond to the message, measuring clicks on the company Web site and blog, and tracking the kinds of buyers who sign up for company offers.

"This kind of messaging development process is critical, because our elevator speech is like our compass," Volpe says. "It helps us to make decisions. While it takes time to get to the messaging, it is worth the effort. Our next step is to refine the HubSpot elevator speech even further into an even shorter statement of a few words that we can use as a tagline."

We find it fascinating that many times the most powerful ideas are developed through collaboration between an organization and a trusted adviser. In a typical scenario, representatives of a company do the hard work of interviewing buyers about market problems and developing their affinity mapping, much like Mike Volpe did at HubSpot. Then, at the time when the elevator speech and the powerful idea are ready to be developed, someone from the outside is called in to help, because the outsider brings a fresh perspective. Here's an example of what we mean.

What's Your Powerful Idea?

 Steve Cohen grew up in affluent Westchester County, where he learned magic from his great-uncle, who had studied under the renowned Harry Houdini. As Cohen was getting started in the world of professional magic, he lamented that people treated all magicians as interchangeable commodities who could be hired on the cheap for their kids' birthday parties. Without seeing him perform, people just didn't understand that he was one of the country's great sleight of hand artists. They'd ask him questions like "Do you fold balloon animals?" and "My daughter is having a Bat Mitzvah on Sunday. Will you do it for $500?" His pride and his wallet were suffering, so Cohen decided to call in positioning expert Mark Levy to help him develop and articulate powerful ideas about his magic.[5]

To come up with his position, Levy informally interviewed Cohen over the course of a month. "We'd be hanging out and I'd ask him about his first performance, his favorite magic trick, and the people he enjoyed performing for most," Levy says. "I'd also watch Steve's shows, and I'd ask audience members about their favorite moments."

As Levy gathered a great deal of information about Cohen, a few key elements were converging to form a powerful idea. "Steve grew up near Chappaqua, NY, which is a very wealthy community," Levy says. "He learned to perform for people who, at times, can be demanding: people with money." In fact, Levy had discovered Cohen's distinctive competence—he was comfortable performing in front of the rich and famous and had done so since the age of ten. "Not everyone knows how to entertain affluent people, who have a lot of options on how to spend their time and money," Levy says. "Steve, though, wasn't exploiting this talent. He'd do shows for anyone who called, and his fees were middle-class affordable, no matter who called."

Levy then drilled down into Cohen's distinctive competence. "I asked about the famous people he performed for and Steve gave me a list. Many on the list were celebrities and movie stars, like Michael J. Fox," Levy says. "But buried in it were some interesting names, such as David Rockefeller, Andy Grove, and Jack Welch. All these names had at least one notable thing in common: they weren't just rich, they were insanely rich."

Levy put all those pieces together and realized that Cohen's best position would be as a performer for the super rich. "As obvious as that sounds, no magic performer was in that space," Levy says. "Other performers were billing themselves as the funniest, or the edgiest, or the flashiest, or the coolest. Or adept at performing at trade shows, or at parties, or for children, or at functions, or they were the best at a specific kind of magic. But no one was focusing on people with insane amounts of money and clout."

The powerful idea that resulted from all of this? *The Millionaires' Magician, Entertainment for Exclusive Events.*

"When Mark first developed my brand identity, 'The Millionaires' Magician,' I fought him tooth and nail," Cohen says. "I was scared it was exclusionary and would frighten people away."

Fortunately Cohen took Levy's advice, because he now commands fees of $10,000 to $25,000 per gig—many times what he was making on the birthday party circuit. In 2005, Cohen made $1 million performing for such people as Martha Stewart, New York City Mayor Michael Bloomberg, and Paul Fireman, the former chief executive of Reebok. The Millionaires' Magician has a weekly gig at the Waldorf–Astoria Hotel in New York and often lives the lifestyle of the rich and famous. For example, he frequently flies on his clients' private jets to gigs at their vacation houses in places like Aspen and Switzerland. He's been profiled in the *New York Times* and other newspapers and on TV for shows such as the *CBS Evening News* and the *Today Show*. Cohen appeared in *Forbes* magazine's 2005 special issue about the 400 richest people in the world. "The article's angle? 'Who do these richest people get to entertain them? Why, Steve Cohen, The Millionaires' Magician','' says Levy.

The transformation of Cohen's business based on the powerful idea of the Millionaires' Magician has changed his life. "I've raised my private-show fee by 2,000 percent and often turn away bookings because my schedule is so full," he says. "I've performed throughout the world, including Lisbon, London, Japan, and Paris. And I've so much business that I had to hire a staff to manage my publicity and bookings." Cohen even signed a deal to write a book for HarperCollins called *Win the Crowd*, and is working on a television special.

All from the power of a few simple words: *The Millionaires' Magician.*

These Guys Understand Me!

As a buyer of products and services, you've probably encountered a number of tuned in organizations. And it's likely that your first encounter was with a concept or even just a phrase the organization presented. It may have caused you to think, "Finally! These guys get my problems, and I can't wait to do business with them!" The tuned in company articulates these powerful ideas from *your* point of view, getting at the core of your market problems. You instantly realize that you've found an organization with a product or service that you want to purchase. We've experienced a few ideas that were so powerful that we had the feeling someone was reading our minds.

Sometimes these powerful ideas are expressed in advertising. The best television, radio, and print advertising draws from the Tuned In Process and articulates ideas that have been discovered by meeting with and understanding buyers and their problems. Unlike most advertising work, which is plucked out of thin air by agencies who don't understand buyers' problems first, the best ads resonate by nailing the essence of a powerful idea.

Powerful Ideas That Resonate:

+ *"1,000 Songs in Your Pocket"*
+ *"Tastes Great, Less Filling."*
+ *"Can you hear me now?"*
+ *"Where's the Beef?"*
+ *"Stay the course"*
+ *"When It Absolutely, Positively Has to Be There Overnight"*
+ *"The ultimate driving machine"*
+ *"All the news that's fit to print"*

Danger! Vision and Mission Statements

Articulating powerful ideas that resonate with your buyers is a natural step in the process of getting tuned in. The powerful ideas, concepts, and phrases naturally flow from your understanding of buyers and their problems. However what we see far more frequently are organizations that are tuned out and that try to engineer mission statements, corporate vision documents, and poorly executed advertising taglines. Unfortunately, these efforts usually fall flat.

A poorly articulated set of "messages" has the power to turn buyers away from your organization.

When ideas are developed through tuned out thinking, they typically cause buyers to say, "I don't want to work with an organization that doesn't understand me or my problems. I'm going to find someone who gets me."

Most corporate messaging of this tuned out variety results in egotistical mission statements developed based on what's important to the company, not what's important for buyers. The big issue here is that these mission statements do not exist for internal use only; many buyers check out these documents as well. And because they're usually created without a true understanding of market problems, they often read as if written by a committee (because they have been)! Consider this one from Bayer:

Bayer Mission:

"Bayer's products and services are designed to benefit people and improve their quality of life. We have set out to create an enterprise that is keenly focused on its customers, its strengths, its potential and the markets of the future: a top international company renowned for product quality, employee skills, economic performance and innovative strength, and committed to increasing corporate value and achieving sustained growth."[9]

This mission statement from Bayer is similar to many we see every day, and frankly it just makes our heads' hurt. While it might be OK to serve constituents such as employees and shareholders, it doesn't contain the powerful ideas that cause buyers to say: "Wow. I want to do business with these guys!"

As you develop concepts that will resonate, don't forget that each buyer persona may require something different from your organization, since each has a different problem for your organization to solve. There's no doubt that your ideas are more likely to resonate if you develop them for each buyer persona instead of simply relying on a generic set of broad messages for everyone.

Resonate Like a Comedian

What makes comedians funny? They are tuned in. The great comedians understand what resonates with people enough to make them laugh. A really good one-liner is a powerful idea, just like those from FedEx or Apple. While a great product or service idea makes us want to learn more, a great joke idea makes us think and then makes us laugh.[7] Some classics:

+ "First you forget names, then you forget faces. Next you forget to pull your zipper up, and finally you forget to pull it down"—George Burns
+ "Why don't they make the whole plane out of that black box stuff?"—Steven Wright

✦ "Have you ever noticed, in traffic, anybody going slower than you is an idiot, and anyone going faster than you is a maniac?"—George Carlin

✦ "I told my psychiatrist that everyone hates me. He said I was being ridiculous—everyone hasn't met me yet."—Rodney Dangerfield

✦ "You have to stay in shape. My grandmother, she started walking five miles a day when she was sixty. She's ninety-seven today and we don't know where the hell she is."—Ellen Degeneres

✦ "*USA Today* has come out with a new survey: Apparently three out of four people make up 75 percent of the population."—David Letterman

Many comedians have a knack for deep insight into certain demographic groups, and very often it is these same groups who enjoy the comedians' performances and buy their products. The humorous twist resonates because comedians are insightful observers, and the ideas they relate resonate with people inside and out of the group being lampooned.

This is true of Jeff Foxworthy, whose distinctive competence is an uncanny knack for understanding blue-collar southerners and performing "common-man comedy." Widely known for his redneck jokes, Foxworthy goes well beyond that to explore the humor in everyday family interactions and human nature. His 1993 comedy album *You Might Be a Redneck If . . .* topped the charts and sold millions of copies; in fact, he has sold more comedy albums than anyone else ever, and his fans have snapped up a string of twenty-two Foxworthy-authored books.[8] Jeff knows how to get his audience's attention:

> **You Might Be a Redneck If . . .**
>
> *. . . you have a complete set of salad bowls and they all say Cool Whip on the side.*
>
> *. . . you own a home with wheels on it and several cars without.*
>
> *. . . you've ever made change in the offering plate.*
>
> *. . . your neighbors think you're a detective because a cop always brings you home.*
>
> *. . . your working television sits on top of your non-working television.*

By getting tuned in to his audience, and especially the very people he was poking fun at, Foxworthy created humor that resonated and leveraged his unique understanding and perspectives to build a career. He is now host of TV's popular game show *Are You Smarter Than a 5th Grader?*

Treat Every Patient Like the President

Here's one last example of an organization that really knows how to communicate with buyers. When Dr. Eleanor "Connie" Mariano opened her Center for Executive Medicine, she vowed to offer the same standard of care to her patients that is offered to the president of the United States: the best, available seven days a week and around the clock, with a minimum of bureaucratic delay and overseen by a doctor "who knows you and understands your individual needs," as the center's Web site says.[9] Now that's a powerful idea—treat every patient like the president!

Mariano knows firsthand about caring for U.S. presidents. While serving as a rear admiral in the United States Navy, she headed the White House Medical Unit through three administrations. Mariano was the primary care physician for presidents George H.W. Bush, Bill Clinton, and George W. Bush, overseeing each president's yearly physical (and briefing the world press on the results), performing routine check-ins and check-ups, and mobilizing emergency teams of specialists (such as the one she assembled on just a day's notice to travel with Clinton to Helsinki for a summit with then–Russian President Boris N. Yeltsin, less than two weeks after an operation to repair damage to his knee).

After leaving the White House for the Mayo Clinic, Mariano tuned in to people's problems with their existing health-care options. Although she worked at one of the best medical facilities in the country, she learned that patients there still felt like they were being treated as part of a standardized care machine. Doctors often saw dozens of patients per day, and the interactions were brief, impersonal, and largely limited to a packaged set of services. While at Mayo, Mariano began a study of how physicians operated their businesses, meeting with hundreds of patients to get tuned in to their needs and preferences.

"After meeting with hundreds of patients, I became convinced that we needed to bring back the notion of the local doctor who really cared about patient care," Mariano says. "When I met with a group of potential investors for the business, I told them that I believed passionately in this notion and talked about all the barriers we would break down that were getting in the way of this fundamental purpose. I was shocked when several of them walked up to me personally afterwards and wrote checks from their own personal accounts to encourage me to start the practice right now."

The Center for Executive Medicine is built with the market problems of the busy executive buyer persona in mind. The powerful idea Mariano articulates—treat every patient like the president of the United States—is much more than a hollow tagline or trumped-up mission statement. The idea permeates every aspect of her practice:

- ✦ The president's time is valuable, and he (or she) never waits. When you arrive at Mariano's Center for Executive Medicine, you're greeted at the door, offered a cup of coffee, and shown immediately to Dr. Mariano.
- ✦ The president doesn't have time for paperwork and shouldn't have to go through the excruciating process of reentering personal data for each visit. Mariano's practice is fully automated and paperless. Patients are never stopped for payment or asked to provide written updates on details like insurance.
- ✦ The president expects to be treated as a VIP. Mariano ensures that she and her staff are always attentive to their patients. They know patients by name, they know their histories, and they know their families.
- ✦ The president can pick any doctor he wants. Mariano knows that the quality of the experience is key to finding and keeping patients, so she mixes diagnostic questions with questions like "What would make your life better?" and "How can we help you achieve that goal?"
- ✦ When the president wants to see a doctor, he sees a doctor, day or night. Mariano is only a phone call away, whether you are nearby, on the road, or even overseas.
- ✦ The president expects a relationship and wants to talk to one individual about his important and private medical issues.

Mariano provides that same level of service for her patients, working as the leader of a distributed medical team that includes hospitals, specialists, and pharmacies. Patients make one call to Dr. Mariano, and she takes care of the rest.

"I never questioned a call in the middle of the night when I was working for the president," Mariano says. She now applies the exact same principles to her practice. "My goal is to ask the right questions to ascertain what the problem is, and then take all of the issues of dealing with that problem away from them."

As a result of getting tuned in to her marketplace and articulating the powerful idea of health care that is as good as the president's, the Center for Executive Medicine is now one of the fastest-growing, most profitable practices in the Phoenix metropolitan area.

"When I was taking care of the president, it was funny because he'd come in for a visit and we'd have a full team of specialists in the waiting room for my diagnosis to see if they were needed or not," Mariano says. "Imagine that, the doctors were waiting on the patient! If you treat everyone as if they were the president of the United States, you know exactly what is required. The quality of care has to be superior and you make sure you're developing a relationship built on trust. Translating that level of care to every patient who walks through that door is what we're all about. We tell our patients to expect nothing less."

Chapter Summary

✦ Tuned in organizations identify several powerful ideas—phrases and concepts that your buyers relate to—to communicate with the market.

✦ The most powerful ideas are those that draw directly from your company's distinctive competence and map perfectly to the unresolved problems of your buyer personas.

✦ Be mindful of what you want your buyers to believe about your company and how you solve their problems.

✦ The most powerful ideas for communicating with the market rarely have anything to do with describing what a product or service actually does.

✦ You may need to identify different ideas for communicating with different buyer personas.

✦ The best television, radio, and print advertising draws from the Tuned In Process and articulates the ideas discovered by meeting with buyers to understand their problems.

✦ Examples of powerful ideas include Apple's "1,000 Songs in Your Pocket," Nike's "Just Do It," and FedEx's "When It Absolutely, Positively Has to Be There Overnight."

✦ Many tuned out organizations engineer mission statements, corporate vision documents, and poorly executed advertising taglines that usually fall flat. Avoid creating documents that focus on your company's needs and goals rather than those of your buyers.

CHAPTER

9

Step 6: Establish Authentic Connections

How do we tell our buyers that we've solved their problems so they buy from us?

Barbie, the best-selling fashion doll in the world, was launched in 1959, and Mattel says that one *billion* Barbie dolls have been sold worldwide since then, with another three sold every second. Barbie has always kept up with the times. Her clothes, hobbies, and occupations reflect the changing society that she lives in and the changing interests of the elementary and middle school girls who play with her. In recent years, Barbie has even gone digital, with a Web site "to engage, enchant, and empower girls . . . to be creative and explore their individual interests through a variety of exciting activities, from online art to interactive games."[1] And Barbie.com has done well—as of this writing in October 2007, the Web site is ranked number 1,100 in the world based on traffic.

So how is it that Stardoll, only three short years after its digital launch, could be ranked as the number 386 site in the world based on traffic, have six million unique visitors per month, and enjoy more than double the daily page views of Barbie. com? How could Stardoll, an independent, digital dress-up doll, that started as the hobby site of Scandinavian-born "Liisa," become significantly more popular than Barbie.com?

Simple. Stardoll got tuned in to the "tween" market (girls from eight to twelve years old), and the site delivers what the girls want: community, celebrity, and fashion. Stardoll members access the site in their choice of sixteen languages (including English, German, French, Spanish, Italian, and Chinese), set up a profile to house their virtual doll and clothing collections, and become online friends with others. The people behind the scenes at Stardoll created a breakthrough experience that resonates with girls all over the world, and so they flock to Stardoll over Barbie.com. Girls love that they can dress up virtual versions of stars such as Ashley Tisdale, Stacy Ferguson, Hilary Duff, the Olsen twins, Rihanna, and Hayden Panettiere. They eagerly participate in live chats with idols like Avril Lavigne. And members maintain their very own blogs and photo galleries so they can share their collections with their friends.

Stardoll has established an authentic connection with tween girls by delivering content relating to the things they enjoy, particularly fashion. Every celebrity doll has a wardrobe full of clothes and outfits, and new ones get released each week. The fashion industry has taken note, with cosmetics by Sephora and clothing by Donna Karan's DKNY label now available in virtual form when Stardoll members go shopping on the site. (In setting up the deal, it didn't hurt that Sephora and DKNY both belong to the French business giant LVMH.) Stardoll, backed by venture capital firms Sequoia Capital and Index Ventures, continues to grow quickly. In the three-month period ending October 15, 2007, Stardoll global reach was up 15 percent while Barbie.com was down 1 percent.

Authenticity Beats "Messages" Every Time

As you've worked through the Tuned In Process with us, you've seen how we keep referring back to the critical importance of understanding the market problems of your buyer personas. By "living in your buyers' world," you build deep empathy with your buyers as people instead of relating to them as interchangeable data points. The people behind Stardoll are tuned in to tween girls. They understand what girls enjoy doing, and they created a resonator that provides that kind of experience.

The next step of the process—establishing authentic connections—takes place when your organization communicates with your buyers to show them that you have a product or service worth considering. At this point, you may be saying to yourself, "Isn't that just the stuff we're already doing, like corporate communications, marketing, and public relations?" Well, yes and no. While establishing connections with your buyers is a form of marketing communications, it is *not* the same command-and-control, message-driven, one-way advertising approach that most organizations are used to.

For decades, tuned out companies have focused on two ways of getting noticed: buy your way in with expensive advertising or beg your way in by courting the media.

Marketing people have always operated under the assumption that you had to pay big bucks for TV and radio spots, invest in magazine and newspaper ads, spend on trade shows, billboards, direct mail—all of it interruption marketing. The tuned out company is forced to try to jolt people away from what they are doing and coerce them into paying attention to a message. When a tuned out company fails to understand buyer personas and market problems, the only way to reach people is through big-budget advertising "campaigns." With so many marketers shouting "BUY MY PRODUCT" in increasingly annoying ways, buyers have responded by turning their minds off and ignoring this never-ending barrage of advertising messages. The resulting chain reaction means even more aggressive (and expensive) messages being delivered through even more channels *and reaching even fewer people who care.*

At the same time, tuned out companies also devote huge resources to public relations "campaigns" that focus their attention on mainstream media, attempting to convince magazine, newspaper, radio, and TV journalists to tell their company's story. These massive, risk-prone operations tie up money and time while offering uncertain results. If you're engaged in a "campaign," and it's not military, then you're probably working too hard.

Buy your way in or beg your way in, the basic mistake is the same. The tuned out company lets itself believe that the only way people solve problems is by sitting around and passively waiting for an advertisement or article that delivers just the right information.

The Authentic and Transparent Hospital

Paul Levy is president and CEO of Beth Israel Deaconess Medical Center (a teaching hospital of Harvard Medical School) and he writes the popular blog Running a Hospital. Recognizing that hospitals have many constituents (patients and their families, doctors and staff, the community served by a hospital), Levy uses his blog as an important communications and management tool. Among many other things, Levy posts about clinical data that a hospital sees in virtually real time—things like quality and safety. Running a Hospital has about ten thousand visitors per week.

"As an academic medical center, Beth Israel Deaconess Medical Center is a high-cost part of the medical system," Levy says.[2] "The public has the right to know what they are getting for their money. So what better way to make a case that we're adding value to our public, and to the government agencies that support and regulate us? Why not show what we're doing as a public institution through the blog? This is an exceptionally useful tool as part of the public debate and to hold our own people accountable."

Levy says the blog makes it easier for doctors and employees at the hospital to work together. For example, he posted information gathered at Beth Israel Deaconess Medical Center about ventilator-associated pneumonia that helped to save more than ninety lives.

"People in hospitals are caring and they want to eradicate disease. The blog creates better work because we are not afraid to say what we're doing and how we're helping. We put ourselves under the microscope."

Connecting with Your Buyers Directly[3]

If you've happened to have read David's most recent bestselling book, *The New Rules of Marketing & PR*, or if you follow his blog, you're already familiar with many of the ideas we share in this chapter. You may recall David's riffs on Web content and publishing compelling content, which we draw from in this section.

One of the simplest ways to establish authentic connections is to target specific buyer personas with content and programs that you create especially for them. A vast majority of Web sites utterly fail to do this. They ignore the Web's endless possibilities and fall back on sites that are one-size-fits-all, with the content organized around the way the company categorizes its products or services, not around the types of buyers whose problems are solved by the products and services. Here's a simple test offered by MarketingSherpa: Look at your marketing materials and count the number of times you see the words "we," "us," "our," or your company's name (on your Web site or product collateral, for example). Then count the number of times you see "You" or "Your," or information about your buyer personas. Which count wins? If it's the latter, congratulations, because you are establishing authentic connections with your buyers.

The same thing is true about most companies' marketing communications programs. Without a focus on the buyer, marketers build programs around what the organization wants to say rather than what the buyer needs to hear. The difference between these two approaches (the latter tuned in, the former tuned out) is tremendous, and it's the difference between success and failure for many organizations. Successful companies focus on buyers and the best ways to reach them, and they develop compelling content and programs accordingly. If you've conducted interviews with buyers as part of the Tuned In Process, then you should already have developed buyer persona profiles and know the problems that your product or service solves for each buyer. You should also have identified the powerful ideas that articulate these solutions to your buyer. Now you need to identify the media that your buyers turn to for answers. When they visit Google and other search engines, what words and phrases do they enter? Which blogs, chat rooms, forums, and online news sites do they read? Are they open to viewing audio or video content? Do they attend events or conferences? You need to answer these questions before you continue.

High Flying Communications

We recently attended an air show featuring the United States Navy Blue Angels flight demonstration teams. The Blue Angels (and the Air Force Thunderbirds) are truly impressive, not only for their awesome displays of precision flying, but also because they're a terrific marketing tool. Young people see the six Boeing F/A-18 Hornets zooming in tight formation and many say, "I want to do that too!" The military is tuned in to what gets young people interested in possibly joining.

The ideal approach when trying to establish connections with buyers in person is "show, don't tell." In this example, don't *tell* us it's cool to be in the military, *show* us. A Blue Angels flight demonstration exhibits the sharply honed set of skills necessary to a naval aviator, with displays like the elegant four-plane diamond formation and the headlong wizardry of the squad's pair of solo pilots. The Blue Angels flew nearly seventy air shows at thirty-five locations in the United States during the 2007 season, bringing out more than 17 million spectators.[4] At the show we attended, recruiters were on hand to answer questions and encourage people to join the Navy. And the recruiting stations were jammed with "buyers."

Of course, we don't all have access to hundreds of millions of dollars' worth of air power to demonstrate our companies' capabilities. But every organization can demonstrate, give away, or showcase some aspect of its work in a way that resonates with buyers. And the best way to do this is to be tuned in to what your market values most.

What about your organization? How can you tune in? How can you show people that you're the right choice to do business with? How can you encourage people to join your group, vote for your candidate, buy your product, or donate money to your cause?

Your Buyers Turn First to the Web to Solve Problems

On the speaking circuit, we ask a series of questions to groups of people representing diverse industries, job functions, and regions. All told, we've asked thousands of people the following questions.

In the past month or two, in your personal or professional life, have you:

+ Been to a trade show to solve a problem or research a product?
+ Answered a direct-mail solicitation to solve a problem or research a product?
+ Used a newspaper or magazine, or the radio or TV, to solve a problem or research a product?
+ Used Google or another search engine to solve a problem or research a product?
+ E-mailed a friend, family member, or colleague to solve a problem or research a product? Was the answer that came back a link to a Web site?

How about you? How would you answer this series of questions for your own personal and professional life?

The results of our show-of-hands survey are remarkably consistent over the many diverse groups that we've asked. The first three questions consistently score between 5 percent and 20 percent, while the latter two questions consistently score between 80 percent and 100 percent. How about you? Did you say "no" to the first three questions and "yes" to the last two?

What this data tell us is very important.

Almost everyone turns to the Web to solve problems and research products much more often than they turn to magazines, newspapers, radio, TV, and direct mail. Search engines and "word of *mouse*" (asking friends, family members, and colleagues via e-mail) are the ways people find answers today, both personally and professionally. Buyers search Google, read online portals and news sites, consider bloggers' advice and opinions, pay attention to the links that peers, friends, and colleagues send them, and visit company Web sites.

We can't help but notice a huge disconnect in many companies:

> **While tuned out organizations spend the big bucks on direct mail and advertising, buyers are busy using the Web to make product and service decisions.**

So what's a marketer to do?

The answer is to think like a publisher and create compelling online content in the form of online news releases, blogs, podcasts, YouTube videos, and other online media to reach your buyers directly. Each of these outlets also has an opportunity to go viral, which means others could join up to spread the word about your company.

Think Like a Publisher

At this stage of the Tuned In Process, you must think like a publisher. Develop an editorial plan to reach your buyers with Web content that will help them solve their problems. Your first step might involve creating content-rich Web "landing pages" organized by buyer persona. This does not mean you need to redesign your entire Web site; you can start by just creating some new individual pages, each with specialized content customized for a particular buyer persona. Then include appropriate links to these new pages from your home page.

> **Publish your way in with great content that your buyers want to consume.**

For example, our hypothetical hotel from Chapter 5 would create a content-rich site with pages for each of its buyer personas. A one-size-fits-all hotel Web site that talks about fluffy pillows and tasty shrimp does not appeal to future hotel guests because it doesn't describe how the hotel solves their problems. Here are some examples of the types of content that the hotel might put onto individual landing pages on the site:

+ Information about must-have services like wireless Internet connections and parking options for independent business travelers who make their own decisions about which hotel to stay at.
+ Details on how the hotel will reduce overall costs, minimize paperwork, and centralize billing for company travel departments that cut deals with this hotel chain.
+ Price quotes for group meal options, AV equipment, and the dedicated support staff who will work with organizations that book hotel meeting rooms for conferences, conventions, and seminars.
+ Highlights of the safe, fun, and hassle-free experience offered to vacation travelers, and details about pool hours, kid-friendly facilities, self-service laundry rooms, and the like.
+ All the important particulars required by couples planning a wedding reception, especially information about guest list sizes, menu flexibility, alcohol service, and—a crucial point—reservations and availability.

You can see how the tuned in Web site is quite different from the uniform, product-centric sites that most organizations deploy. Consider Vantage Mobility International (VMI), a manufacturer and distributor of accessible transportation solutions, including minivan conversions, full-size van conversions, platform lifts, scooter and wheelchair lifts, and transfer seats. VMI's products deliver buyers an incredibly powerful experience: freedom.

 What's interesting about the VMI Web[5] site is its focus on very different buyer personas. Unlike a typical site, which just prattles on about products, VMI's has links right from prime real estate at the center of the home page to landing pages that provide valuable information for, and customer quotes from, each buyer persona. Here's how the home page and landing pages make authentic connections with each of the four buyer personas:

Senior/Mature— *"Whether you need to visit the grandkids, check in on a friend or lead the choir—Our wheelchair accessible van and wheelchair lift products give you the freedom."*

Active/Independent— *"There's no stopping you! So, grab your buddies and head out on a road trip, participate in the Bolder Boulder wheelchair race, visit every baseball stadium in North America."*

Caregiver/Assistant— *"Of course our wheelchair lifts make it easy to assist others in one of our custom wheelchair accessible minivans or full-sized wheelchair accessible vans, but they also make it easier to haul furniture, deliver a new washing machine, pickup a big screen TV."*

Parents— *"Families go places! Our full-size wheelchair accessible vans and minivans give you the freedom to experience. So, get out and take your kids to a ball game, explore the country, visit the zoo."*

The buyer personas that VMI communicates with have very different problems that need solving. Those problems are reflected in the way that the company communicates right on the home page and the landing pages.

Once you've built a content-rich Web site, and with your publisher's hat still on, consider additional media your organization can publish on the Web to reach the buyers you've identified. You might create an e-mail newsletter, blog, podcast, or a series of direct-to-consumer news releases focused on problems you know your buyers are interested in. Many tuned in organizations create an editorial plan for each buyer persona in the form of a calendar for the upcoming year. This calendar might coordinate publication dates for new Web site content, an e-book, a blog, and some news releases.

"You Must Unlearn What You Have Learned"[6]

To be successful, you need to unlearn the marketing habit of constantly pitching your product. Instead create information that helps your buyer personas to answer their questions and solve their problems. Your materials (the company Web site, brochures, product and service literature, programs to reach people, and other marketing materials) should all be created from your buyers' perspective. Forget about your products and services and instead work from your buyers' point of view, drawing from the powerful ideas you've already articulated. (See Chapter 8 if you need a refresher on developing ideas that resonate.) You should create materials that show how your organization solves buyer problems, not how your product works. This connection with and focus on buyers should extend to the company's sales professionals (if you have them) and their approach to the marketplace. Are your salespeople so busy selling the merits of your offerings that they forget to find out about the buyers' needs first?

> **Tuned in companies reach people who are eager to buy their products and services without being coerced.**

✦ You must unlearn the habit of interrupting people with "messages." Instead, publish online content they want to consume.
✦ You must unlearn the use of meaningless gobbledygook phrases (such as those used in a typical mission statement). Instead, focus on the problems and needs of your buyer personas.
✦ You must unlearn spin. Instead, understand that people crave authenticity and transparency.
✦ You must unlearn egotism and the desire to force buyers to adapt to your terms. Instead create online content that puts the buyer first.
✦ You must unlearn the assumption that you have to buy access. Instead, create content that goes viral and let millions of people tell your story for you . . . free.

What Do Donkeys Have to Do with Marketing?

Most marketing and communications programs from business-to-business software and technology companies are painfully boring. If some of these companies tried to smile, we think their computer screens would crack. But guess what?

Your buyers, no matter what sort of organization you work for, are people—real people with a sense of fun—not nameless, faceless, corporate drones. Sometimes a bit of the unusual and funny can work wonders.

Steve Kayser, PR manager at Cincom Systems, one of the largest privately held software companies in the world, is a master at establishing connections with his buyers in online marketing and communications, having built the Cincom *Expert Access* eZine from zero to 135,000 subscribers in just a few short years.[7] Cincom is a global company, and *Expert Access* counts subscribers from dozens of countries. It is written for senior-level corporate executives, IT and operations managers, and technology buyer committees.

Humor plays an important role in the publication.

Kayser writes a hugely popular regular feature called "Shoot the Donkey." Wait, donkeys? In business-to-business software company communications? According to Kayser, "Shoot the Donkey" gets its name from a scene (based upon a real-life event) in the movie *Patton* where the U.S. Seventh Army gets critically held up in the heat of battle. The culprit? A cart-pulling donkey that refuses to budge, totally blocking a bridge. Life and death are at stake. An MP struggles with the donkey and the owner, trying to get them out of the way.

The entire U.S. Seventh Army halts for a recalcitrant donkey.

General George Patton then roars up, leaps out of his jeep, whips out his ivory-handled pistol, and shoots the donkey dead. He immediately has the poor creature hurled off the bridge, removing the obstacle. "That classic scene not only revealed Patton's character in a cinematic way but also embodied the great success principle of personally taking decisive action to remove all obstacles to fulfill one's mission," says Kayser.

Patton himself explained it like this: "I didn't like shooting the donkey, but I preferred that to the alternative of having the Luftwaffe arrive to strafe the column and kill large numbers of my men."

Kayser likes taking decisive action too, and he uses humor to remove communications obstacles to fulfill his mission of establishing connections to his buyers. "People like donkeys," he points out. "Look at Shrek's donkey. He's a movie star!"

Can you think of any other B2B software companies that have a "spokes-donkey" like Cincom has? Or can you imagine another company in this traditionally dull and conservative market running a lead article in their online newsletter entitled, "How to Defeat Your Inner Deadbeat . . . In Your Life of Business or in the Business of Life"? Kayser received over 250 e-mails about this story alone. People wrote to tell him how it helped and inspired them. Steve Kayser does all of this and more, and he proves that humor works in the B2B world.

"I like the fact that Cincom *Expert Access* not only creates awareness, but also generates leads and business," Kayser says. "I had one case where I had been e-mailing back and forth with a guy for almost a year—he loved the donkey—and one day he says, 'Oh, by the way, I signed a deal with you guys last week.' I didn't even know he was in the sales cycle. Later the salesperson told me the guy loved the donkey and Cincom *Expert Access* and it was a great business facilitator."

Of course, the publication isn't all fun and games. *Expert Access* delivers valuable information to its customers. Each issue comprises a dozen or so articles and the popular "Ask the Expert" section, where readers' questions are answered by an outside expert—not Cincom employees. The newsletter is so good that it often has a viral marketing effect. Readers share it with friends and colleagues, and the articles get picked up by other publications. All this attention drives additional readers to Cincom's Web site.

Kayser has collected over 300 reader comments, nearly all positive, which he posts online. Many of the comments come from folks with job titles and corporate credentials representative of Cincom's buyer personas—companies like Hewlett-Packard, Northrop Grumman, the Chicago Mercantile Exchange, Allstate, and many others. These comments prove that the newsletter is reaching its targeted buyer personas. One reader commented, "You seem to have an uncanny knack of picking articles that speak directly to problems our company faces."

You can't get any more tuned in than that!

Each month, Cincom *Expert Access* points an average of nearly two thousand potential customers to offers and calls to action, or to additional product and service information on the Cincom Web site. Steve Kayser and his donkey have contributed to Cincom's achieving twenty-one straight years with more than $100 million in revenue—they're the only private software company in the world to attain this lofty feat. Kayser understands his buyer personas and creates authentic connections to them via Cincom *Expert Access*.

Chapter Summary

✦ This step of the process—establishing authentic connections—takes place when your organization communicates with your buyers to show them that you have a product or service worth considering.

✦ While establishing connections with your buyers is a form of marketing communications, it is *not* the same command-and-control, message-driven, one-way advertising approach that most organizations are used to.

✦ One of the simplest ways to establish authentic connections is to target specific buyer personas with content and programs that you create especially for them. Without a focus on the buyer, it's too easy to build programs around what the organization wants to say rather than what the buyer needs to hear. Successful companies focus on buyers and the best ways to reach them, and they develop compelling content and programs accordingly.

✦ People turn to the Web to solve problems and research products much more often than they rely on magazines, newspapers, radio, TV, and direct mail.

✦ Search engines and "word of mouse" (asking friends, family members, and colleagues via e-mail) are the ways people find answers today, both personally and professionally. Buyers search Google, read online portals and news sites, consider bloggers' advice and opinions, pay attention to the links that peers, friends, and colleagues send them, and visit company Web sites.

✦ Tuned in companies think like a publisher and create compelling online content in the form of online news releases, blogs, podcasts, YouTube videos, and other online media to reach their buyers directly. Each of these forms of media also has an opportunity to go viral, which means others could join up to spread the word about your company.

10

 # Cultivate a Tuned In Culture

How do we ensure our organization is tuned in?

The Apple iPod, first released in 2001, had one of the most talked-about product introductions of the past decade. Many people have theories for why the iPod has been so successful (100 million units sold as of the end of March 2007).[1] Pundits point to such factors as Steve Jobs' brilliance, the power of the company's advertising, and the elegance of the product itself. While these elements are all important to the mix, the Apple's iPod success can be explained more simply. If you've followed the *Tuned In* journey from the opening chapters, we're sure you now know why the iPod has resonated so well with buyers. *Apple tuned in!* Professionals at Apple applied each of the six steps of the Tuned In Process to create and launch the resonator that is the iPod. As we've studied the iPod and other wildly successful products and services, we realize that for a true resonator to break out of the pack and achieve market-changing status, each one of the six steps of the Tuned In Process needs attention.

Before the iPod came along, portable digital music players were crammed with features and functions and buttons, and they sported software that was difficult to master. Apple CEO Steve Jobs, back at the helm of the company he cofounded, led a development effort focused on solving a problem in the marketplace—the need for a portable digital music player that *was easy to use.*

The breakthrough iPod experience was about much more than "better" hardware. Since its launch through the time of this writing, here are things we've identified that Apple has done to contribute to the iPod becoming a resonator.

- ✦ Apple applied its elegant design philosophy to everything— the portable unit itself, the look and feel of the interface, the simple ergonomics, and even the beautiful packaging.
- ✦ The white "ear buds" served to create a cult-like status for iPod users, because everyone else's headsets and cables were black.
- ✦ The simple functionality required little documentation to be included in the box.
- ✦ The iPod was easy to learn how to use. The wheel-based interface is more intuitive than the buttons other players had at the time.
- ✦ Apple launched a sister product, iTunes, to eliminate many of the obstacles to downloading and organizing digital music.
- ✦ Apple forged partnerships with record labels and others in the music industry and launched the iTunes Store, where customers legally purchase copyrighted music for $0.99 per song.
- ✦ The iTunes Store was later expanded to include audiobooks and radio stations as well as video, including movies and TV shows.
- ✦ iTunes embraced "podcasts"—consumer-generated audio content that is syndicated to people's iPods (and computers). Later, "vodcasts" (video podcasts) and ring tones were also added.
- ✦ The powerful idea used in iPod advertising was exceedingly simple: "1,000 Songs in Your Pocket."
- ✦ The iPod TV commercials, which featured colorful shadows of people dancing to popular songs, became popular. In fact,

millions of people *choose* to watch them on YouTube. A number of consumer-generated versions have been posted to YouTube as well, driving the viral marketing effects of the advertising.

✦ Even the sales experience is carefully designed to fit the company's image. Apple operates nearly two hundred retail stores that sport clean, sharp lines and plenty of stations for trying out the products.

✦ In the business-to-business world, the company's trade show and exhibition booths display only the Apple logo—no distracting "messages."

Now, just six short years after its introduction, the iPod is one of the world's most popular consumer brands and enjoys 72 percent market share. We predict continued success as Apple's corporate culture makes a habit of being tuned in and developing products that resonate.

Each Step Is Important

How successful would the iPod have been if Apple ignored any one of the steps of the Tuned In Process? Imagine, for instance, what would have happened if the company had not learned about the real problems buyers had accessing music and therefore had neglected to create the iTunes interface? Without the white ear buds, would the cult of the iPod have developed as rapidly?

As we reflect on the iPod and its success, we're reminded of two products that resonated with buyers but whose makers neglected one or more of the six steps in our process. In one case, the company built a product that resonated with one market, but the company missed other markets for lack of understanding buyer personas. In the other, the company was unable to establish connections with buyers because it focused on interruption-based advertising techniques.

The first example was the Segway two-wheeled electric transportation device. When it was launched in 2001, the Segway generated tremendous media attention. Much of the early buzz revolved around the idea that the Segway would replace cars; some commentators predicted that it would completely transform the way people live in cities. The Segway's early marketing was targeted at a "city dweller" buyer persona, but the product never seemed to catch on with this group, mainly because of the high price of $5,000 per unit. However, other buyer personas were happy to pay the $5,000 price and roughly 23,500 units sold through September 2006.[2] For example, Segways are used by airport personnel to move quickly and quietly inside large terminals, by police in some towns, and by tourists for sightseeing at popular destinations. Had it done buyer persona research, Segway Inc. could have saved itself time, money, and frustration.

 The second was TiVo, a brand of digital video recorder (DVR) for recording television programs.[3] As you probably know, TiVo works much like a video-cassette recorder but records onto an internal hard drive. TiVo resonated with buyers because it allowed them easy control over when they could watch their favorite shows. In marketing the product, the company could have focused on that but didn't. Instead it tried drawing attention to all of TiVo's features, such as fast-forwarding through commercials. Buyers were confused, leaving word of mouth to supply the message the company should have been promoting—use TiVo and watching late-night talk shows in the morning becomes a snap, as does recording any show you want to see and viewing it when you want. Today, although TiVo has more than 4.2 million subscribers, the company has struggled to grow and become profitable, and in fact reported losses for fiscal 2005, 2006, and 2007. We wonder how much more successful TiVo would have been if they had created a powerful idea for the TiVo, an equivalent to the iPod's "1,000 Songs in Your Pocket."

Segway and TiVo are great examples of products that fell just short of being resonators because the companies behind them failed to execute one of our six steps. Sure, *TiVo* is now a verb synonymous with recording, but it has underperformed compared to what it could have been if the company had articulated the idea in a more powerful way. When organizations focus on the entire Tuned In Process and use it as the guiding principle of their businesses, they begin to build a corporate culture that fosters success. People at all levels of companies like Apple use tuned in language and think outside the organization first.

Saying "NO"

As the Segway and TiVo examples show, each step of the Tuned In Process is important and will help focus your company's attention on market problems and buyer personas instead of egotistical nonsense. In fact, once they have tuned in, many organizations think of the process as a permanent filter for analyzing opportunities and decisions, their ongoing guide to when to say "no."

+ When somebody in your company (even the boss) wants to build a new product or service, the Tuned In Process suggests questions to ask first. What problems does this product solve? For what buyer personas does it solve these problems? If the person with the idea has not done the research, use the Tuned In Process as a filter and say "no."
+ When an agency or media partner wants you to invest in an advertising or promotion initiative, the Tuned In Process helps you identify the powerful ideas that you need to articulate to buyers to help you develop authentic connections with them. If the proposed initiative doesn't fit, just say no. We know people who have used the Tuned In Process to help investors and board members understand why the company does not advertise in famous business magazines.
+ The Tuned In Process is also an important early part of annual budget planning, helping to identify where human and financial resources should be deployed—and where they should *not* be deployed!

Sales and Distribution That Resonates

Launching your resonator effectively requires that you choose a winning sales and distribution strategy. While a comprehensive look at sales and distribution is beyond the scope of this book, we do suggest that you consider the Tuned In Process when making these decisions. Before you make a final determination on sales and distribution, look at the market problems that your product solves and which buyer personas it solves them for. Oftentimes, tuned in organizations will identify alternatives to the supposedly tried-and-true sales and distribution strategies.

+ For many consumer product companies, mass retailers like Wal-Mart or Costco make up a coveted sales channel. But as we learned in Chapter 5, Nalgene bottles are sold only via the company's own Web site and in specialty retail stores.
+ Mark Batterson of National Community Church, whom we met in Chapter 7, chose to "distribute" church services in movie theaters instead of traditional church buildings.
+ At around the same time that it launched the iPod (2001), Apple began to build its own Apple stores in cities and shopping malls around the United States. The company now has nearly two hundred such locations where consumers can try out the latest products.
+ Unlike other rental car companies, which maintain physical offices staffed by attendees, Zipcar (from Chapter 3) unleashed its offering using an innovative Web-based membership system and card-activated vehicle access, eliminating the need for customers to visit an office.

Tuned In Employees

As your organization practices the tuned in approach to doing business, everyone begins to live and breathe the concepts involved. Eventually, getting and staying tuned in become a part of the corporate culture, with staffers and management alike challenging the old ways of doing things. Even if your entire organization isn't completely tuned in, employees and departments can be. Employees who understand the tuned in philosophy know what market problems their organization solves, and so they learn to do what's right for buyers. Call it "tuned in customer service." We see it more often than you might think.

Recently, a colleague took his family of four on a Florida vacation via Southwest Airlines. As they approached the check-in counter, his two teenage daughters attempted to heft their jam-packed suitcases onto the scale. Grimacing and grunting, they asked for their dad's help.

As he no doubt feared, both girls' bags were significantly over the Southwest Airlines weight limit. For each ticketed customer,

Southwest allows three checked pieces at no cost as long as each individual piece weighs fifty pounds or less. (There are also size restrictions.)[4]

"I'm sorry, your bags are over the limit," said the check-in agent. "You're going to have to pay an extra fee if you bring those bags as is." The clerk explained the overweight policy: bags weighing from 51 to 70 pounds are accepted for a charge of $25 per bag, and items weighing from 71 to 100 pounds are accepted for a charge of $50 per item. Any item weighing more than a hundred pounds must be shipped as air cargo. The girls' bags weighed in at around eighty pounds each.

So far, this story is no different from similar encounters that occur thousands of times a day at airport check-in counters all over the world. But Southwest isn't just any airline. Southwest is tuned in to its buyer personas and their problems. And the company is also keenly aware of the need to establish authentic connections with customers to drive word-of-mouth buzz about the company.

"You only have one bag each and we allow three per person," the counter agent continued. "How about this? I can sell you both Southwest Airlines duffel bags for $25 each, and you can transfer some of your belongings into them to get each bag below the weight limit."

Our colleague was amazed. He was prepared to pay $100 to Southwest Airlines to take the bags packed with excess weight. But instead he purchased two nifty Southwest Airlines duffel bags for half that amount and still got all of his girls' belongings to Florida.

"And now we carry those duffels on all of our trips," he says. "The Southwest Airlines logo is getting lots of mileage with our family."

Here's a company that not only cares about its customers, but also understands how to generate buzz. Our colleague says he's told this story dozens of times. He also says he's a loyal Southwest Airlines customer as a result.

Get Tuned In Right Now

Getting tuned in seems easy at first, until you realize that you need to change your habits. Hopefully, you're asking, "OK, but what do I need to do now?" Here are some important first steps that will help you get started. As you begin to live the tuned in culture, these things will become natural for you.

Top Ten Actions to Create a Tuned In Culture:

1. Get out of your office and talk with buyers about their unresolved problems.
2. Identify your buyer personas. In order to make them real for you and your colleagues, name each buyer persona, build a profile for each, and cut a representative photo from a magazine to represent them.
3. Define your distinctive competence. Make certain everyone on your team understands what it is.
4. Don't go to an internal meeting if you're only going to give your own opinion. Instead, be the person who goes to the meeting armed with data.
5. Always ask where "facts" come from, to disqualify mere opinions from your decision-making process.
6. Map your products and services on the Tuned-In Impact-Continuum. Build a plan to increase the impact.
7. Don't talk about what your product or service does. Tell customers which of their problems the product or service will solve.
8. Count the number of times you say "our" and "we" on your Web site. Write for your buyers by using "you "and "your" instead.
9. Remove corporate gobbledygook, such as mission statements, from your external communications.
10. Become a thought leader in your market and industry.

You Can Do It Too

We've talked a great deal about how Apple used the Tuned In Process to make the iPod an incredible success. You might be tempted to think that achieving this sort of success is beyond your organization's abilities. But consider this: in 1993, before the introduction of the iPod, Apple (under its then chairman, John Scully) made a great noise about the release of the Newton MessagePad, a product that many within the company thought would reinvent personal computing.[5] On the heels of two huge successes (the Apple II and the Macintosh), the notion seemed plausible. With the hype and buzz that have become a hallmark of an Apple product launch, early Newton advertising proclaimed, "The astonishing new invention that has room for your whole world but fits in your pocket. It manages your days, your names, and your numbers. It sends faxes and replaces your pager. It makes writing readable. It can draw even if you can't. It talks to computers and printers. And what you don't know, there's a good chance it does." Wow. But what was the response? Well, in April 2007 *Computerworld* nominated the Apple Newton as one of the 21 biggest technology flops of all time. The product was not built to solve problems, and therefore it did not resonate with buyers. In 1993, Apple was tuned out and many people wondered if the company would survive at all.

Yet Apple would go on to introduce the iPod, a tuned in product if ever there was one. The company has been tremendously successful since then, with company stock soaring from about $8 a share in January 2001 (pre-iPod) to $180 as of this writing in October 2007. For Apple, the value of getting tuned in was a twenty-two-fold increase in company stock price!

If a large public company the size of Apple can execute a complete turnaround and get tuned in, so can your organization. It doesn't matter if you're part of a big company or a small one. You could work for a nonprofit, a government agency, or as an independent consultant. Or you could be a political candidate, a member of a rock band, or the pastor of a church. *The Tuned In Process applies to you.* In the next and final chapter, we'll introduce you to several more tuned in people and the resonators they've created. We're absolutely convinced that any organization can replicate their success.

Chapter Summary

+ The best way to develop a product or service that truly resonates is to carry out each of the six steps in the Tuned In
  Process.
+ Each step is important for focusing the attention of your organization on market problems and buyer personas, not
  egotistical nonsense.
+ Sometimes a product that ought to resonate will fail to capture the attention of buyer personas because of a reliance on
  old-style "messaging" techniques that focus on product attributes rather than powerful ideas your buyers can relate to.
+ The Tuned In Process can be used as a filter to help you decide what initiatives to pursue and when to say no.
+ Unleashing your resonator requires that you consider the
  market problems your product solves and who it solves them
  for *before* you make a final determination about sales and
  distribution.
+ Oftentimes, tuned in organizations will identify alternatives
  to the supposedly tried-and-true sales and distribution
  strategies.
+ Getting and staying tuned in should become a part of your
  organizational culture. Employees who practice the tuned
  in philosophy understand what market problems their organization solves and learn to do what's right for buyers.
+ Any organization can create a resonator, including yours!

11

Unleash Your Resonator

How do we become and remain a market leader?

E ver heard of Joseph Swan?
    What if we told you that he invented and patented an incandescent lamp with a filament made from carbonized paper in a partial vacuum: in other words, the world's first electric light bulb.[1]

"What a minute," you say. "Didn't Edison invent the light bulb?" That's what we thought too. But it turns out, in this case, that Edison wasn't so much innovative as tuned in. What he did best was connect to the market problem of bringing light into homes. He was the first to show the invention in action, because, as the owner of a power company that later became known as General Electric, he had easy access to enough electricity to support a proper demonstration of the world-changing capabilities of electric light. Edison knew that without power, a light bulb doesn't solve anyone's problems—it's just a glass bulb with a filament. Edison lost a patent dispute in court over the light bulb, but he went down in history as the invention's father because he was the one who made it a break-through experience.

Thanks for hanging in there with us and making it to this final chapter! We want you to have success like Thomas Edison and Steve Jobs and Mark Batterson of National Community Church, and we know the Tuned In Process can help you get there. Sure, a focus on innovation may yield your own version of the light bulb. But if you don't develop, market, and distribute your invention the right way, you're more likely to end up like the hapless Joseph Swan than the famous and successful Thomas Edison.

By now, you know all you need to know about the Tuned In Process and how to apply it. But there may still be a problem for some of you. When we run seminars and give speeches on the ideas you've read about in *Tuned In*, many people are excited about transforming their businesses. They understand the power of the process and the enormous benefit of getting tuned in. If that describes you, great! But we often encounter another (smaller) group of people who are still a bit skeptical. Often these folks work in nontraditional organizations, and they want to believe that the Tuned In Process doesn't apply to them. They say things like, "Well this sounds good if you're a big company like Apple or an Internet-based offering like Stardoll, but we're a _____." (Feel free to fill in the blank with "nonprofit," "government agency," "rock band," "bookstore," "recent college graduate looking for a job," and so on.) We get some push back because some people don't immediately see a benefit for someone in their particular situation.

Getting tuned in offers benefits to all kinds of people (including you) and all kinds of organizations (including yours). Let's take a look at some:

No-hassle airports: Many airports in the United States have tuned in to the market problem of passenger pickup and now offer "cell-phone parking lots" to simplify the process.[2] Drivers wait in these lots for arriving passengers to claim luggage and reach the terminal sidewalk. The arrivals make a quick call, and their rides pick them up in minutes. Los Angeles International, Seattle-Tacoma International, Baltimore/Washington International, Birmingham International in Alabama, Palm Beach International in Florida, and Chicago's O'Hare International are among those that have a cell-phone parking lot located just a few minutes' drive from arrival terminals. And cell phone lots don't just solve problems for arriving passengers and their rides; the lots also reduce traffic by eliminating the practices of repeated loops, slow drive-bys, and illegal parking, all of which were commonplace just a few years ago.

Go ahead, make it viral: Unlike virtually all other bands of the era, the Grateful Dead, a popular jam band that began some thirty years of touring in the 1960s, allowed concertgoers to record their live shows. The band even sold "taper section" tickets for where the acoustics were best. Tapers were free to make copies of the live recordings to give away and swap with others (but were not allowed to sell their tapes or make copies of studio recordings). As a result, the music of the Grateful Dead was shared far and wide, leading to more and more fans who wanted to see the live shows. This tuned in policy helped the Dead become one of the most profitable touring acts in rock history.

Shorten the distance between you and your customer: Have you ever been stuck in a restaurant waiting for a table to open up? We recently found ourselves facing a wait of more than an hour and expected to either be pointed to the restaurant's bar or handed one of those big clunky buzzers that force you to stay in the restaurant because of their short signal range. So imagine our delight when we were told the restaurant had deployed a new service from Somtu MMS (mobile messaging system) that texts, "Your table will be ready in ten minutes" to your mobile device. Cool. We could then visit the nearby shops while we waited. When we discussed this product, we realized that although we were users of this technology, we were not the buyer persona. Restaurant management has an unresolved problem and is willing to pay money for this technology, but we diners are just the beneficiaries. Wanting to learn more, we went to the company's Web site, where we found this powerful idea: *The shortest distance between you and your customers.*[3]

When you have to raise prices: Each time the U.S. Postal Service raises the price of a first-class stamp, consumers can't use the old stamp without buying a few cents' worth of additional postage. This is a real problem that frustrates many people and creates long lines at the stamp window around the time of each price increase. The Service tuned in to one of their buyer personas (the folks in the lines waiting to buy two-cent stamps) and the problems they face (wasting time) and introduced the "Forever Stamp" in the spring of 2007.[4] The Forever Stamp, which costs the same as first class postage at the time it is purchased, is always good for mailing first-class letters no matter when it is used—this year, next year, or twenty years from now. Forever Stamps resonate with customers, who are thrilled that they can buy a stash of stamps and not worry about future price increases making their lives difficult. Sometimes when we tell this story, we get push back from people who say that the Postal Service is tuned out. Maybe so. However, we think that the Forever Stamp is utterly tuned in. They found a problem and solved it with a brilliant resonator. It is remarkable when a tuned in product comes from a tuned out organization.

 **It takes money to build a village:** In recent years, one of the hottest new areas of finance has been microcredit: small loans to impoverished people in developing countries. Entrepreneurs and nonprofits first tuned in to this market problem, providing loans of $50 to $500 to help people buy necessities like an ox for tilling a field, irrigation equipment for watering crops, a building to house a small shop selling basic goods in a village. The rate of default was remarkably low, and soon mainstream financial institutions jumped into the market. Microcredit proved to be such a resonator for helping to raise standards of living and creating jobs in poor countries that the United Nations declared 2005 the International Year of Microcredit.[5]

 **Farm Aid faithful:** Willie Nelson, Neil Young, and John Mellencamp organized the first Farm Aid concert in 1985 to raise awareness about the loss of family farms and to raise funds to keep farm families on their land. The nonprofit Farm Aid organization stages America's longest-running annual concert event, uniting farmers, artists, music fans, and concerned citizens to promote a strong and resilient family farm system.[6] But the concert event lasts only one day, and Farm Aid has a year-round mission promoting food from family farms. The organization effectively reaches out to diverse constituents, including

those who help support the mission with donations, music fans who eagerly await the live concert in September, and the farmers who are helped throughout the year. To generate interest in the 2006 concert among music fans and particularly the Farm Aid faithful (who go to the concerts each year, belong to the fan club, and buy logo gear such as T-shirts), the organization ran a contest called "Top of the Haystack" to seek out the ultimate Farm Aid fan, who would win an all-expenses-paid trip to the concert and two front row seats. Using a "microsite" (a Web site tailored to one buyer persona) music fans and the Farm Aid faithful uploaded photos and essays to win the title of top Farm Aid fan. The Top of the Haystack site was a huge viral marketing success, generating millions of visits and driving paid subscriptions to the Farm Aid Fan Club to a 73 percent increase from the year before. As a result of focusing on buyer personas, the Farm Aid organization has raised more than $30 million to support its goal of helping farmers thrive.

The joy of painting: For decades, paint has been sold in difficult-to-open metal cans. But check out your local paint store to see the result of Dutch Boy getting tuned in to its market. Instead of selling paint in the messy and unwieldy traditional paint can that everybody else uses, Dutch Boy sells paint in a convenient plastic container with an easy-grip handle and twist-open spout. Soon after the breakthrough product experience was introduced, Dutch Boy doubled its sales.[7]

Sports is entertainment: The Entertainment and Sports Programming Network (ESPN) burst onto the scene in 1979 with a resonator for those sports fanatics with an insatiable desire for live action and smart analysis. On ESPN, sports isn't just news, it's an entertainment experience that appeals to more than 89 million people who have made the network their source for sports.[8] By getting tuned in, ESPN discovered how to connect to what their buyers value most: hard-hitting analysis and plain fun. On ESPN, athletes aren't just numbers on jerseys, they are characters with clever nicknames (like Joseph "Live and Let" Addai or Bert "Be Home" Blyleven) in an ongoing drama delivered by a network connecting with its core audience. As viewers flocked to the new channel, so did the advertisers who wanted to reach them.

ESPN now ranks second in paid advertising dollars per minute, behind only Nickelodeon.

In search of the Holy Grail: As the leading source for difficult-to-find and out-of-print books about space exploration, Boggs Space-Books has carved out a thought leadership position that drives business.[9] In mid-2007, Boggs put out a call to collectors to nominate their entries for the "Top 20 holy grails of space book collecting, those books which are the rarest and most desirable." Although owners Donald and Tamara Boggs had their own ideas for the list, they tuned in to their customers' opinions in a two-step online voting process. The first nomination step yielded a surprising 250 entries, so they divided the final customer voting into two categories: signed books (many by astronauts) and the rare books that contribute the most to an understanding of spaceflight. This is a great example of how to establish authentic connections with buyers. In the process, the lists have no doubt led many fans to covet a new rare or signed book, which they can purchase from, you guessed it, Boggs SpaceBooks.

The Power of Getting Tuned In

As we've mentioned several times, executives and staff at many companies already think they are tuned in. Hey, the mission statement even says so! When we go into these organizations and actually measure the things that people do all day, we inevitably witness problems and missed opportunities that originate from inside-out thinking (think Apple Newton) rather than outside-in thinking (think iPod). In other words, companies are ineffective because their field groups and customer-facing organizations spend more time postulating and pontificating around scenarios that support their offerings than listening and learning about problems their customers actually have (and are willing to spend money to solve).

There are some real measurements that may be used to assess how tuned in your organization is right now. We challenge you to objectively answer the following questions. If you answer "yes" to all of them, congratulations, because you're already tuned in!

✦ Does someone other than sales routinely visit buyers and potential customers?

✦ When you have a meeting with a buyer, do you spend most of
the time listening instead of talking?

✦ Are your product and services created to solve problems in
the market?

✦ Are your communications based on the specific and quanti-
fied problems of a well-defined market and buyer?

✦ Does your Web site focus on market problems faced by your
buyer personas and solutions to those problems (instead of
egotistical nonsense about your products and the "mission"
and "vision" of your company)?

Tuned in companies answer these questions in the affirmative.

The Tuned In Career

What's so fascinating about the tuned in approach is that once you understand the fundamentals of being tuned in, you can apply them to
all aspects of your career. When you're tuned in
to your boss's needs, you manage him or her in a
way that resonates and therefore the two of you
have a better relationship. When you're tuned in to the industries
and roles that are best for you, you make the right career decisions.

We've become fascinated with the concept of the tuned in resume. Think for a moment about how you painstakingly put together your resume when you were looking for work. It was all about you,
wasn't it? Did you think about the market problems of the hiring
manager first? Probably not. Yet when we think about the resumes
that we find intriguing when we hire new people, we realize they're
always the ones where candidates spoke to us using the language we
wanted to hear and identified the problems that hiring that person
would solve. In fact, many people aren't even using resumes any
more. Keeping a constantly updated career blog is a great tuned in
idea not only to track and measure your own progress, but also to
show potential employers how you can solve their problems.

And getting tuned in works for organizations who want to hire
the best staff as well. Heather Hamilton's role as staffing manager

for strategic talent acquisition, community, and research at Microsoft is to fill the potential employee pipeline with great marketing job candidates.[10] Rather than following the traditional recruiter path of scouring Monster, CareerBuilder, and other job sites, she blogs, speaks at industry events, and gives interviews to media outlets including the *Wall Street Journal,* the *New York Times,* and *Fast Company.* She has made herself a thought leader in recruiting circles, especially among recruiters looking for tuned in ideas for finding great employees. Today, marketers looking to work for Microsoft know the person to contact is Heather Hamilton, not some faceless HR Department.

The Tuned In Leader

So many of the companies we meet with focus on the wrong things. People work like crazy to implement sales and marketing programs before they understand buyers and their problems. They develop "messages" and create advertising campaigns and PR slogans. They hire great people to promote products and create market push. They egotistically talk only about their products (not buyers' problems). These companies stay busy but they don't resonate.

Tuned in leaders work differently from the pack. Tuned in leaders don't obsess about the competition; instead they obsess about market problems. Tuned in leaders understand the complete picture of those market problems *before* creating product experiences. Tuned in leaders learn how to develop product experiences by meeting and understanding people in the marketplace and observing how they do business.

The most important thing tuned in leaders do is to live in the potential customer's world, especially by interviewing and studying potential customers. The tuned in leader develops a corporate culture that works to achieve the following objectives:

+ Find unresolved problems in the marketplace.
+ Know prospective customers and their problems better than they know themselves.
+ Build a business case based on quantifying the impact of the offering in the market.

✦ Create breakthrough product experiences that solve market problems by leveraging the organization's distinctive competence.

✦ Clearly understand and articulate the powerful ideas that resonate for buyers.

✦ Establish connections by communicating to a well-defined set of prospective customers the way the customers want to be communicated with.

✦ Distribute the product experience in the way that makes it easy for people to buy.

When we went back and reviewed notes from our discussions with dozens of CEOs and analyzed the survey data we collected, we found some striking similarities among the companies that are winning in the marketplace. So pragmatic were these tuned in ideas that most of the successful CEOs we talked with treated them as nothing more unusual than looking both ways before crossing the street. These maxims seemed to help the tuned in companies operate with a sense of comfort and confidence, in stark contrasts to the tuned out companies, which seemed to be constantly struggling.

Get Tuned In Today

Your momentum is working against you. It is easier to stay tuned out. It's so darn simple to waltz into internal meetings at your company and talk about your opinions. It's so fun to build a product because it's cool. It's so easy to hire an advertising agency to invent messages for you. But as you've seen in these pages, getting tuned in is more likely to lead to success than these other strategies are.

As we said in Chapter 2, we think of getting tuned in as important because you counteract what we've termed the "gravitational force" that tends to pull companies back to a "normal state" of being tuned out. Getting tuned in is like riding a bicycle—it is scary at first and a strange feeling, but once you've practiced a bit it's easy and natural. People are genuinely afraid to get out in front of people and get tuned in to their problems. And leaders are worried that they might find things wrong with their businesses. So they stay in the office and tune out.

You don't need to be the CEO to get tuned in. As you begin to trust the market to deliver the signals to you, as you learn to discover the deep and real connections that your market values most, as you focus on your buyers and their problems, you'll become tuned in. And as the market sends out messages, you'll pick them up to create your very own resonator. Your business, and you yourself, will be in a better place.

We have taught people in thousands of companies how to implement the Tuned In Process, so we have seen how it produces success. The Tuned In Process was the basis for transforming these companies and the individuals who work for them. What our customers usually find out is that it's not about being smarter, better funded, or endowed with an abundance of unique assets . . . it's about systematically following a proven path to success.

Now it's your turn.

Chapter Summary

+ By now, you know all you need to know about the Tuned In Process and how to apply it.
+ Getting tuned in offers benefits to all kinds of people (including you) and all kinds of organizations (including yours). Companies large and small, entrepreneurs, government agencies and nonprofits, even churches, rock bands, and politicians transform their businesses by getting tuned in.
+ There are some real measurements that may be used to assess how tuned in your organization is right now, and we challenge you to objectively answer the questions we pose.
+ What's so fascinating about the tuned in approach is that once you understand the fundamentals of being tuned in, you can apply them to all aspects of your career: managing your boss, writing a resume that resonates, even making the right career decisions.
+ Tuned in leaders work differently from the pack. The most important thing tuned in leaders do is to live in the potential customer's world, especially by interviewing and studying potential customers.
+ Your momentum is working against you because it is just easier to stay tuned out.
+ We think of getting and staying tuned in as being like a diet. As anyone who has dieted knows, it is not easy to change your eating habits. However, diets work when they become such an integral part of your daily routine that you don't even need to think about it anymore. It's the same with getting tuned in.
+ We know from teaching the Tuned In Process to people in thousands of companies that it produces success.
+ What our customers usually find out is that it's not about being smarter, better funded, or endowed with an abundance of unique assets . . . it's about systematically following a proven path to success.
+ Now it's your turn!

Notes

Chapter 1. Why Didn't We Think of That?

1. Train-line hotels: David lived in Tokyo from 1987 to 1993 and took the train to work every day.

2. Wellbe Hotels: see http://www.wellbe.co.jp/

3. David's book: *The New Rules of Marketing & PR*, John Wiley & Sons, Inc. © 2007

4. Russell Shaw: We interviewed Russell in October 2007. The Russell Shaw Group's Web site is at www.nohasslelisting.com.

5. "1,000 songs": This line was used in the first TV commercial for the iPod and Steve Jobs made a specific reference to the value of a thousand songs in the launch presentation he gave in 2001, adding, "This is a quantum leap because for most people this is their entire music library. This is huge!"

6. "Absolutely, Positively": See www.fedex.com/cgi-bin/global_legal .cgi?cc=us&sc=/legal/copyright/au.html.

7. The Tuned In Organization: Richard Branson was profiled in *Inc.* magazine's "26 Most Fascinating Entrepreneurs" in March 2005. Grant Griffiths' Kansas Family & Divorce Lawyer blog, at the time of this writing, is the number one listing in Google when searching for "Kansas family law." See www.kansasfamilylawblog.com for his blog. In the announcement for Habitat for Humanity's two hundred thousandth home, they note it took twenty-four years to build the first hundred thousand homes and only five years to build the second hundred thousand. See www.habitat.org/celebrate _build/press/200k_house_announcement.aspx. Barack Obama's "savvy Internet campaign" was described in the *San Francisco Chronicle* on April 5, 2007 (see www.sfgate.com/cgi-bin/article.cgi?f=/c/a/2007/04/05/OBAMA. TMP) and in *Time* on July 5, 2007 (see www.time.com/time/magazine/ article/0,9171,1640402,00.html). The Barack Obama Web site shows more than 1 million contributors. See www.barackobama.com See www.thedailyshow.com

andwww.medialifemagazine.com/artman2/publish/Cable_20/Hefty_bounces
_for_Stewart_and_Colbert.asp for Jon Stewart's *The Daily Show*. See www
.lakewood.com for Joel Osteen's Lakewood Church.

8. What led to *Tuned In:* Market-driven organizations were studied by
George S. Day and Prakash Nedungadi in "Managerial Representations of
Competitive Advantage," *Journal of Marketing* 58 (1994): 40. Software Minds
researched product-management best practices for Pragmatic Marketing in
2004, and we conducted interviews with thirty technology CEOs in 2006.

9. Surveys: Pragmatic Marketing conducts annual surveys to understand the current professional life of product managers and marketers, and
the effectiveness of corporate strategies at technology companies. For 2007
over 3,500 responses were received. The results from these and previous
surveys underpin the arguments in this book.

Chapter 2. Tuned Out . . . and Just Guessing

1. Building a better mousetrap: See www.victorpest.com/canada/
history.asp.

2. Dollar coin: John P. Caskey and Simon St. Laurent, "The Susan B.
Anthony Dollar and the Theory of Coin/note Substitutions," *Journal of
Money, Credit, and Banking* 26 (1994). Jillian Leifer "The Susan B. Anthony
Dollar: A retrospective" *The Numismatist,* official publication of the American
Numismatic Association, October 1998. The formal name of the vending
machine lobby is National Automatic Merchandising Association (NAMA).

3. "Where's the Beef": See www.wendys.com/legal.jsp for Wendy's
copyright on this phrase.

4. Internet refrigerator: "No Need for PCs with Intelligent Fridges,"
LG Electronics press release issued by PR Connections, December 13, 2000.
Today, due to advances in electronics, the product's cost is half that of the
original (although still many times the average cost of most refrigerators
currently available).

5. Sony and DRM: This issue was first reported on October 31, 2005,
by Mark Russinovich on his blog and attracted worldwide attention on the
Internet and in other media. (See blogs.technet.com/MarkRussinovich).
Sony BMG provided information to consumers and a way to trade CDs for
new ones. (See blog.sonymusic.com/sonybmg/archives/111505.html).
Soon after Texas, California, and New York sued Sony BMG, law student
Mark Lyon started a blog to track Sony BMG XCP rootkit lawsuits. (See
www.sonysuit.com.)

6. 1–800 phone numbers: See "Spelling Trouble" by Chris Sewell, *Telephony*, October 14, 2002, available at icbtollfree.com/pressetc/telephonyarticle10142002.html.

Chapter 3. Get Tuned In

1. Avis: For more on the history of Avis, see www.avis.com/AvisWeb/JSP/global/en/aboutavis/corp_info/historical_chronology.jsp.

2. Zipcar: We interviewed Robin Chase in November 2007. Other useful information came from "Part-Time Wheels: City Dwellers Share Cars through New Service" by Heidi B. Perlman, Associated Press, http://www.onlineathens.com/stories/072000/new_0720000010.shtml; and from "Scott Griffith: Zipping Ahead" by Lisa van der Pool, *Boston Business Journal*, August 24, 2007; and "Zipcar is shifting into high gear as market widens" by Yoon S. Byun, *The Boston Globe*, January 13, 2008. http://www.boston.com/cars/news/articles/2008/01/13/zipcar_is_shifting_into_higher_gear_as_market_widens/. Numerous customer video testimonials are on the Internet, including "A Zipcar Story" www.youtube.com/watch?v=nQPZfmuKDos, "Foggy Evening with Zipcar" www.youtube.com/watch?v=VUL1li6H1B8, and "Surprise Visit Via Zipcar" www.youtube.com/watch?v=ViA2wKkOI3E.

Chapter 4. Step 1: Find Unresolved Problems

1. TV remote control: "New Survey Details America's Relationship with TV Remote Control," Philips Consumer Electronics Company press release issued via PRNewswire, September 22, 1994. Philips is the company behind Magnavox products. http://www.langston.com/Fun_People/1994/1994AWM.html

2. Volvo: See www.volvocars.com/experience/safety.htm.

3. Quicken: We interviewed Steve Bennett, CEO of Intuit, in October 2007.

4. Self-service gas pumps: "Marketing Mistakes in New Business Ventures" by Howard Upton, *Spirit* magazine, April 1991, page 27.

5. Blogs: David Sifry, the founder and chairman of Technorati, wrote "The State of the Live Web" in April 2007, saying Technorati tracks over seventy million blogs. See www.sifry.com/alerts/archives/000493.html.

6. Disneyland: For an analysis of how Disney tuned in, see *Spinning Disney's World: Memories of a Magic Kingdom Press Agent* by Charles Ridgway, published by Intrepid Traveler, 2007.

Chapter 5. Step 2: Understand Buyer Personas

1. Nalgene bottles: We interviewed Eric Hansen, Marketing Manager, in September 2007.

Information for people in the laboratory market is available at www.nalgenelabware.com, for general consumers www.nalgene -outdoor.com, and for the green buyer at www.refillnotlandfill.org.

2. Wedding planning: We interviewed David Liu, CEO and cofounder of The Knot, in November 2007. See www.theknot.com for the wedding planning site and www.thenest.com for the "Nesties" community site.

3. Security Moms: See www.time.com/time/columnist/klein/article/ 0,9565,421149,00.html.

4. Surfer camera: We interviewed Nicholas Woodman, founder and CEO of GoPro in November 2007. Customer uploaded videos taken with their GoPro camera can be seen at gopro.vsocial.com or www.goprocamera .com.

Chapter 6. Step 3: Quantify the Impact

1. StubHub: The following press releases give details and can be found via Web search engines: "StubHub (an eBay Company) and MLB Advanced Media Forge Long-Term Online Secondary Ticketing Partnership," August 2, 2007; "eBay to Acquire Online Tickets Marketplace StubHub," January 10, 2007; and "StubHub Approaches Ten Millionth Ticket Sale," October 5, 2007.

2. BlackBerry: "Research In Motion Reports Preliminary Fourth Quarter and Year-End Results for Fiscal 2007, Status Update, April 11, 2007 and SEC filings for years 2005–2007," Research In Motion news releases can be found at www.rim.com/news/press/.

3. Bill Me Later: The introduction to this section was synthesized from the following articles: "Big Plastic's Online Challenger" by Peter Burrows, *BusinessWeek*, December 30, 2005 (see www.businessweek.com/technology/ content/dec2005/tc20051230_391101.htm); "Credit Card Fraud Bedevils Web" by Craig Bicknell, Wired.com, April 2, 1999 (see www.wired.com/ techbiz/media/news/1999/04/18904); and "Credit Card Killer" by Erika

Brown, Forbes.com, December 11, 2006 (see members.forbes.com/forbes/ 2006/1211/068.html).

For online merchants who offer Bill Me Later, see shopping.billmelater .com/merchants/index.html. The Inc. 5000 profile of Bill Me Later is at www.inc.com/inc5000/2007/company-profile.html?id=200700060.

Chapter 7. Step 4: Create Breakthrough Experiences

1. National Community Church: The church's Web site is at theaterchurch.com. Mark Batterson's "Evotional" blog can be found at www.evotional.com, and Mark and his team are profiled at theaterchurch .com/about/staff. We interviewed Mark Batterson in October, 2006.

2. Boeing Dreamliner: See www.boeing.com/commercial/787family; "How Boeing Put the Dream in Dreamliner" by Douglas Gantenbein, *Smithsonian*, September 2007 at www.airspacemag .com/issues/2007/september/dreamliner.php; and www.boeing .com/randy/archives/2005/07/the_magic_is_ba.html.

3. Distinctive competence: For FedEx, see www.fedex.com/hn_eng lish/about/facts.html and www.alexa.com/data/details/main/fedex. com. Volvo discusses its approach to safety at www.volvocars.com/experience/ safety.htm. Interlink describes the RemotePoint Navigator 2.4 at www.smklink.com/index.php?id=Mzk1. For more on Zipcar, see www .zipcar.com; for Cityside Garage, www.citysidegarage.com.

4. Cold Stone Creamery: We interviewed Doug Ducey in October 2007 who provided us with financial information. For more on the company, see www.coldstonecreamery.com/about/press_room.html.

Chapter 8. Step 5: Articulate Powerful Ideas

1. Bush White House slogans: See www.whitehouse.gov/news/ releases/2006/08/20060830–10.html.

2. Buyer persona: For FedEx reliability, see www.fedex.com/us/ about/unitedstates/advertising. For Volvo safety, see www.volvocars.com/ experience/safety.htm.

3. U.S. Army: See www.goarmy.com.

4. HubSpot: The company shares its vision at www.hubspot.com/ internet-marketing-company. Mike Volpe's career is summarized at www .hubspot.com/company/management/mike-volpe.

5. "The Millionaires' Magician": We interviewed Mark Levy in November 2007 and Levy communicated with Steve Cohen as we prepared the manuscript. See "Magician to the Rich" by Matthew Miller at www .forbes.com/forbes/2005/1010/060.html; Steve Cohen's Web site at www.chambermagic.com; and Mark Levy's site at www.levyinnovation.com.

6. Bayer: See the company's mission statement. at www.bayer.com/ en/bayer-mission-statement.pdfx.

7. Resonate Like a Comedian: See www.comedy-zone.net.

8. Jeff Foxworthy: See www.jefffoxworthy.com and http://www .brainyquote.com/quotes/authors/j/jeff_foxworthy.html.

9. Treat Every Patient Like the President: We interviewed Dr. Eleanor Mariano in October 2007. See also www.drcmariano.com.

Chapter 9. Step 6: Establish Authentic Connections

1. Stardoll: Barbie's mission can be found at barbie.everythinggirl. com/parents/mission.asp. Web traffic rankings can vary over time and by different measurement systems. For this book we used the current information at www.alexa.com. "Donna Karan, Sephora to Sell in Stardoll Web World" by Michele Gershberg, Reuters, September 26, 2007, can be found at www.reuters.com/article/internetNews/idUSN2545791320070926. For more on Stardoll, see http://www.stardoll.com/en.

2. Beth Israel Deaconess Medical Center: We interviewed W. Paul Levy, president and CEO of Beth Israel Deaconess Medical Center, in November 2007. His blog post on ventilator-associated pneumonia is at runningahospital.blogspot.com/2007/01/reducing-ventilator-associated .html.

3. Connect with Your Buyers Directly: David's blog is at www.webin know.com. MarketingSherpa's site is at www.marketingsherpa.com.

4. Blue Angels: See www.blueangels.navy.mil.

5. VMI: See www.vantagemobility.com.

6. "Unlearn What You Have Learned": We find this quote from Yoda perfect for describing the challenge marketers face when dealing with the "New Rules of Marketing." See fragme.blogspot.com/2006/10/star-wars-yoda-quotes.html.

7. Shoot the Donkey: We interviewed Cincom's PR manager, Steve Kayser, in November 2007. For the Cincom Expert Access eZine, see www.cincom.com/us/eng/expert-access/index.jsp. Reader comments

can be viewed at www.cincom.com/us/eng/expert-access/readerreviews/ index.jsp?loc=usa.

Chapter 10. Cultivate a Tuned In Culture

1. iPod: For the announcement of one hundred million units sold, see www.apple.com/pr/library/2007/04/09ipod.html. For currently available material in the iTunes store, see www.apple.com/itunes/store. For a list of retail stores, see www.apple.com/retail/storelist. For news on market share, see macdailynews.com/index.php/weblog/comments/12374/.

2. Segway: For information on the vehicles' use by government agencies, see www.segway.com/police-government/customers.php. For numbers sold through September 2006, see www.cpsc.gov/cpscpub/prerel/ prhtml06/06258.html.

3. TiVo: See www.tivo.com/whatistivo/index.html.

4. Southwest Airlines: For baggage limits, see www.southwest.com/ travel_center/baggage.html.

5. Newton: For a description, see www.news.com/The-history-of -Apple/2009-1001_3-201295.html. Apple's own Web site contains no references to the Newton product line! For a list of the 21 biggest technology flops, see www.computerworld.com/action/article.do?command=viewArticle Basic&articleId=9012345&pageNumber=1. For Apple's stock price from before the iPod to October 2007, see finance.yahoo.com/q/hp?s=AAPL& a=00&b=1&c=2001&d=09&e=31&f=2007&g=m.

Chapter 11. Unleash Your Resonator

1. Light bulb: Joseph Swan was an English physicist and chemist who obtained a patent in 1860 for the electric light bulb. Thomas Edison later purchased this patent. See www.thehistoryof.net/the-history-of-the-light -bulb.html.

2. Cell phone parking lots: See www.wisegeek.com/what-are-cell -phone-parking-lots.htm and www.concierge.com/cntraveler/blogs/perrin post/2007/09/airport-cellpho.html.

3. Restaurant waiting: See www.somtumms.com.

4. Forever Stamp: See www.usps.com/prices/prices_forever.htm.

5. Microcredit: See www.un.org/News/Press/docs/2004/dev2492 .doc.htm.

6. Farm Aid: For details on the success of Farm Aid in raising funds, see www.wnyc.org/news/articles/85301, www.farmaid.org/site/c.qlI5IhNVJsE/ b.2723609/k.C8F1/About_Us.htm, and www.farmaid.org/site/c.qlI5IhNVJsE/ b.2739785/apps/s/content.asp?ct=4457185 for details of the success of Farm Aid in raising funds. For the "Top of the Haystack" contest site, see topofthehaystack.ning.com.

7. Paint: For information on the success of the new packaging, see www.packagingdigest.com/whitepaper/track.php?id=170, www.robertfalls. com/case_studies/dutchboy.html, and ewweb.com/mag/electric_nurture _renegade_ideas.

8. ESPN: For information on the full range of services currently offered by ESPN see www.hearstcorp.com/entertainment/property/ ent_espn.html.

9. Books: See www.boggsspace.com.

10. Heather Hamilton: For her One Louder blog, see blogs.msdn .com/heatherleigh/default.aspx.

Acknowledgments

We have been very fortunate to have so many people care about this project, offering their time and thoughts on how to make it special, willingly and without any expectation of something in return. More than two hundred fifty people made material contributions. Without their help, we have no doubt the enclosed would stand much less chance of resonating with you. Their selflessness and keen insights are what make putting these things together a special endeavor.

We'd like to offer our special thanks and gratitude to:

- ✦ Our team at Pragmatic Marketing (www.pragmaticmarketing .com), for their dedication in refining our thoughts and ensuring the quality of this book, especially Kristyn Benmoussa, Graham Joyce, Michelle Conlon, Steve Johnson, Chellie Buzzeo, and Amy Maenle for bringing this all together in a first-class way.
- ✦ Our agents, Bill Gladstone and Ming Russell at Waterside Productions (www.waterside.com), for expertly aligning our partnerships based on our goals for this book.
- ✦ The team at Wiley (www.wiley.com)—Matt Holt, Kim Dayman, Jessica Campilango, Shannon Vargo, Cynthia Shannon, Lori Sayde-Mehrtens, Christine Kim, Kim A. Nir, and their colleagues for constant enthusiasm about the project.
- ✦ Meg La Borde and Ray Bard at Bard Publishing (www. bardpublishing.com), for working with us during the formative stages of the book, recognizing the true value of what we were intending, and steering us to the focus of *Tuned In*.

+ Kyle Matthew Oliver for reading every word of the early manuscript and for making it much better with sound advice and practical suggestions.
+ Our expert book launch team including David Wilk at Booktrix (www.booktrix.com) and Mark Fortier at Fortier Public Relations (www. Fortierpr.com).

The following people kindly subjected themselves to our many questions and probing during several review cycles. Their ideas are reflected in the book:

+ Mark Levy (www.levyinnovation.com)
+ Mark Roberts (www.boycepensions.com)
+ Steve Johnson (www.productmarketing.com)
+ Kevin Myers (www.imemories.com)
+ Doug Nicholas (www.greentreepartners.com)
+ Greg Strouse (www.executiveondemand.blogspot.com)
+ Phil Toole (www.mountainvalleychurch.org)
+ Adele Revella (www.buyerpersona.com)
+ Dr. Connie Mariano (www.drcmariano.com)
+ Doug Ducey (www.imemories.com)

We're also indebted to the product management associations around the world that connected with us and allowed us to test the Tuned In concept in their forums:

+ Atlanta Tech Product Management Association: groups.yahoo .com/group/atpma
+ Austin Product Marketing and Management: groups.yahoo .com/group/AustinPMMForum
+ Australia Product Management Association: groups.yahoo .com/group/AustraliaPMA
+ Boston Product Management Association: www.bostonproducts .org
+ British Columbia Technology Industry Association: www.bctia .org/Connections/Product_Management_Group/
+ Calgary Product Management Association: groups.yahoo .com/group/CalgaryProductManagementAssociation
+ India Product Management Forum: finance.groups.yahoo .com/group/IPMF

✦ Israel Product Management Association: www.ilpma.org
✦ Puget Sound Product Management Forum: groups.yahoo .com/group/PSPM
✦ San Diego Product Management Association: www.sdpma.org
✦ Silicon Valley Product Marketing Association: www.svpma.org
✦ Tampa   Bay   PMA: finance.groups.yahoo.com/group/ tampabaypma/
✦ Toronto Product Management Association: www.tpma.ca
✦ Triangle Product Marketing Association: groups.yahoo.com/ group/trianglepma
✦ UK Product Marketing Forum: groups.yahoo.com/group/ UK_Product_Marketing

Finally, we would also like to thank the hundreds of individuals who took the time to be interviewed by us and the many bloggers who added to the conversations and "webinars" around the Tuned In concept. You all greatly enhanced our view of the concept. In particular, the incredible voices of the people listed below made writing this book much easier. Check out their companies and blogs!

✦ Steve Bennett (www.intuit.com)
✦ Jim Davis (www.sas.com)
✦ Roger Helms (www.helmsbriscoe.com)
✦ Jim Basille (www.rim.com)
✦ Jim Malcolm (www.rosettaexploration.com)
✦ Keith Boswell (www.strikeiron.com)
✦ Michael Harris (www.adapt.com)
✦ Rich Corley (www.akorri.com)
✦ Steve Goldstein (www.alacrablog.com)
✦ Marc Sokol (www.jkbcapital.com)
✦ Fred Amoroso (www.macrovision.com)
✦ Mark Bonfigli (www.dealer.com)
✦ Matthew Rizai (www.asu.edu)
✦ Don Bulens (www.equallogic.com)
✦ Dick Costello (www.feedburner.com)
✦ Wolfgang Koester (www.fireapps.com)
✦ Tom Aley (www.generateinc.com)
✦ Chris Morrison (www.barvision.com)

- Ian Bonner (www.inxight.com)
- Cliff Pollan (www.lumigent.com)
- Larry Schwartz (www.newstex.com)
- Dave Simbari (www.optum.org)
- Barry Bealer (www.reallysi.com)
- Armando Viteri (www.ameritege.com)
- Pat Sullivan (www.freshbrew.com)
- Dee Rambeau (www.thefuelteam.com)
- Tim Butler (www.unimax.com)
- Mike Grandinetti (www.virtualiron.com)
- John Carrington (www.websense.com)
- Christophe Fabre (www.axway.com)
- Chris Hoover (www.chrishoover.org)
- Bob Corrigan (acknak.blogspot.com)
- Laura Ries (ries.typepad.com/ries_blog)
- Seth Godin (sethgodin.typepad.com)
- Art Petty (artpettyonmanagement.typepad.com/bestpractices)
- Geoffrey Moore (geoffmoore.blogs.com)
- Nilofer Merchant (www.winmarkets.com)
- Kristin Zhivago (www.revenuejournal.com)
- Guy Kawasaki (blog.guykawasaki.com)
- Anne Pauker Kreitzberg (www.leadersintheknow.com)
- Heather Hamilton (blogs.msdn.com/heatherleigh)
- Alan Armstrong, Ethan Henry, and Saeed Khan (onproductmanagement.wordpress.com)
- Scott Sehlhorst (tynerblain.com/blog)
- Gopal Shenoy (gopalshenoy.wordpress.com)
- Joel Spolsky (www.joelonsoftware.com)
- Roger Cauvin (cauvin.blogspot.com)
- The Cranky Product Manager (www.crankypm.com)
- Jeff Lash (www.goodproductmanager.com)
- Brad Baldwin (www.rockymountainnews.com)
- William Hsu (hitchhiker.blogsome.com)
- Paul Young (www.productbeautiful.com)
- Rich Mironov (www.mironov.com)
- Robin Lowry, Peter Ganza, Stewart Rogers, Allan Levson, and Julian Byrne (www.featureplan.com/community)
- Bonnie Rind (www.productpersonas.com)
- Ivan Chalif (www.theproductologist.com)

+ Rob Grady (www.robgrady.com)
+ Scott Gatz (www.scottgatz.com)
+ James Robertson (www.cincomsmalltalk.com/blog/blogView)
+ Bikram Gupta (www.bikramgupta.com)
+ Bruce McCarthy (www.userdriven.org/blog)
+ Gopal Shenoy (gopalshenoy.wordpress.com)
+ Adam Bullied (writethatdown.com)
+ Paul Dunay (buzzmarketingfortech.blogspot.com)
+ Charlene Li (blogs.forrester.com/charleneli)
+ John Jantsch (www.ducttapemarketing.com/blog)
+ Dharmesh Shah, Brian Halligan, and Mike Volpe (blog .hubspot.com)
+ John Dodds (makemarketinghistory.blogspot.com/index .html)
+ Adrienne Tan and Nick Coster (www.brainmates.com.au)
+ Ardath Albee (marketinginteractions.typepad.com)
+ Douglas Karr (www.douglaskarr.com)
+ Sean Branagan, John Whiteside, and Maureen Rogers (opinionatedmarketers.blogspot.com)
+ Michael Stelzner (www.writingwhitepapers.com/blog)
+ Debbie Weil (www.blogwriteforceos.com)
+ Eric Sink (www.ericsink.com)
+ Johanna Rothman (www.jrothman.com/blog/mpd)
+ Garr Reynolds (www.presentationzen.com/presentationzen)
+ Jill Konrath (sellingtobigcompanies.blogs.com)
+ Bob Schmonsees (blog.valuemapping.net)
+ Grant Kitching (grantsproductmanagementblog.blogspot .com)
+ John Moore (brandautopsy.typepad.com)
+ Gustavo Arizpe (www.areastrategica.com)
+ Mark Howell (www.strategycentral.org)
+ Brother Maynard (subversiveinfluence.com/wordpress)
+ Jeff Giesener (thegies.typepad.com)
+ Marty Taylor Collins (martycollinsblog.spaces.live.com)
+ Paul Dunay (buzzmarketingfortech.blogspot.com)
+ Tom Hackelman (xeroxmarketingsolutions.blogspot.com)
+ Kevin McGrew (www.techbiznewmedia.com/blog)
+ Amitai Givertz (amitaigivertz.blogspot.com)
+ Derek Lee (www.symantec.com)

- ✦ Ryan Hunter (www.newmerix.com)
- ✦ Michael Fischler (www.markitek.com)
- ✦ Don Jarrell (www.digitalthinkinginc.com)
- ✦ Paul Wilson (www.sungard.com)
- ✦ Dan Nottingham (www.kronos.com)
- ✦ April Benetollo (www.daxko.com)
- ✦ Jennifer Cambern (www.rsmes.com)
- ✦ Avni Rambhia (www.arxan.com)
- ✦ Clif Kranish (www.informationbuilders.com)
- ✦ Jeanne Strepacki (www.forrester.com)
- ✦ Tom Wood (www.activant.com)
- ✦ David Adams (www.premiereglobal.com)
- ✦ Wayne Dong (www.freescale.com)
- ✦ Ryan Martens (www.rallydev.com)
- ✦ Robert Duffner (www.ibm.com)
- ✦ Todd Radtke (www.pearson.com)
- ✦ Gene Villeneuve (www.cognos.com)
- ✦ Sue Holub (www.checkfree.com)

Index

About the Authors

Craig Stull is the founder and CEO of Pragmatic Marketing and the developer of the framework that the company uses to provide training and consulting services for creating tuned in businesses. He has more than two decades of experience in the strategic role of product management, specializing in new-product launches, turnarounds, positioning, naming, and potential-client needs identification. Prior to starting Pragmatic Marketing, Craig was vice president of marketing at three large software companies, Legent, Viasoft, and UCCEL where his career was equally divided between product marketing, sales, and technology. This unique combination of skills gives him sensitivity to the full life cycle of building winning products and services. *Tuned In* is his first book. Craig is a graduate of Roger Williams College with a bachelor's degree in business administration. He lives in Scottsdale, Arizona, with his wife, Karen, and their daughter, Olivia.

Phil Myers is the president of Pragmatic Marketing and a writer, speaker, and consultant on the subject of tuned in leadership strategies. Before joining Pragmatic, Phil was a CEO or senior management leader at three start-ups that grew into market leaders—Cyclone Commerce, SalesLogix, and Novadigm. He has managed two successful initial public offerings and launched seven products that became category leaders. As president of Pragmatic Marketing, Myers is responsible for global business operations that serve three thousand technology firms. He also consults with executive teams, keynotes events, and serves on a variety of technology industry boards. *Tuned In* is his first book. Phil is a graduate of the Pennsylvania State University with both a bachelor's and master's degree in business administration. He lives in Scottsdale, Arizona, with his wife, Diane, and their three children—Blair, Courtney, and Logan.

**D**avid Meerman Scott is the bestselling author of *The New Rules of Marketing and PR* and the creator of the Pragmatic Marketing seminar called The New Rules of Marketing. He is a frequent keynote speaker at conferences around the world. For most of his career, David worked in the online news business. He was vice president of marketing at NewsEdge Corporation and Asia marketing director for Knight-Ridder Financial. He has also held senior management positions at an e-commerce company, been a clerk on a Wall Street bond-trading desk, and acted in Japanese television commercials. *Tuned In* is his fourth book. A graduate of Kenyon College, David has lived in New York, Tokyo, and Hong Kong. He lives in Boston with his wife, Yukari, and their daughter, Allison.

Check out the authors' blog at www.TunedInBlog.com

About Pragmatic Marketing

Pragmatic Marketing provides training and consulting services that enable our clients to create tuned in products, services, and businesses. More than 45,000 individuals at over 3,000 companies have been trained in the disciplines we teach, adopting our framework as a standard methodology for product management and marketing. Our portfolio of services includes more than a dozen seminars; consulting that spans workshops, coaching, and complete project implementation; and a thriving online community that serves more than 50,000 monthly visitors.

Founded in 1993, the business was inspired by a problem we'd observed in many firms . . . namely, the trouble they had building products people *wanted* to buy. In the technology industry we served, there was a good bit of innovation going on to attract early adopters, but real "hits" were few and far between. Our training and service offerings are designed specifically to increase that success rate.

The Pragmatic Marketing Framework

The Pragmatic Marketing Framework organizes thirty-seven essential activities we observed in bringing a new product from its formative stages through development to market into a system that is easy-to-understand and implement—from strategic to tactical. We've been pleasantly surprised how well it resonates in the market. For the last ten years, we've watched companies take our framework (which many call "The Grid") and standardize their operations around it—posting copies on the walls in their offices and using it as a methodology for organizing the company to become more market driven.

Everyone—from product managers to developers to marketers to salespeople and eventually even executives—seem to embrace the concepts we teach as "the right way to do marketing." We have taken note and expanded our offerings to include full life-cycle support with training and services to work with our customers to implement these concepts. We publish a magazine every other month (*The Pragmatic Marketer*) and provide an extensive online resource center with tips, techniques, and reference information.

Many of our customers comment on how aptly named the company and the framework are. Both are, well, very *pragmatic*. There is nothing in what we do that makes you want to get out your textbooks to verify or conduct a new research project to find the holes in it. These simple, proven techniques are organized in a way that makes everyone who embraces them more successful in what they do, every day.

Today, our team conducts hundreds of public and private seminars each year, on-site workshops and consulting projects, and many online events for our members and visitors. We've been recognized twice by *Inc.* magazine as one of the fastest-growing private companies, most recently in 2007. We've been profitable every year, with 80 percent of our new business coming from referrals and 90 percent customer satisfaction ratings. Pragmatic Marketing is a global organization with customers in the United States, Australia, Canada, England, Finland, France, Germany, Hong Kong, India, Japan, Singapore, and South Africa. Many make a major commitment to standardize under the Pragmatic Marketing Framework by requiring that all newly hired product management and marketing employees attend training. Two recent milestones stand as testament to the success of this framework: we announced our forty-five thousandth person trained and our eight thousandth person to be Pragmatic Marketing certified. The Tuned In Process and its processes are the core of what we do.

Next Steps

We welcome the opportunity to work with you or your business to provide more about the "how" of getting tuned in, and we are actively looking for partnerships and programs that can bring the Tuned In Process, and the core of what we do, into the industries we studied in writing this book (from real estate to retail to ministries). Visit us at www.tunedinbook.com to learn more and participate on our blog to help us learn what works (and what doesn't), as you put the Tuned In Process into action.

We know from experience that only one thing is certain and that's the inexorable nature of change. We want to keep our concept fresh and we welcome all of the interactions with you as they evolve.